HOPE-LIGHT.

CW01272211

I trust this book has found you for a reason

Katie Jones

Chronically Awesome

Chronically Awesome by Katie Rose Jones

Published by Katie Rose Jones

www.hope-light.co.uk

Copyright © 2024 Katie Rose Jones

All rights reserved.

No portion of this book may be reproduced in any form without written permission from the publisher or author, except as permitted by copyright law. For permissions contact the author: info@hope-light.co.uk, social media @HopeLightUK.

While the publisher and author have used their best efforts in preparing this book, they make no representations or warranties with respect to the accuracy or completeness of the contents of this book and specifically disclaim any implied warranties of merchantability or fitness for a particular purpose. The advice and strategies contained herein may not be suitable for your situation. The information provided in this book should not be treated as a substitute for any medical or professional advice. You should consult with a professional when appropriate. Neither the publisher nor the author shall be liable for any loss of profit or any other commercial damages, including but not limited to special, incidental, consequential, personal, or other damages.

Editor: Sian Smith

Book Cover by Katie Rose Jones

Illustrations by Katie Rose Jones

Paperback ISBN: 978-1-0686762-0-8

eBook ISBN: 978-1-0686762-1-5

DEDICATION

This book is dedicated to my husband, Lee Roy Jones. There are not enough words in the world to describe my gratitude to this man and all the crap he has had to live through with me.
And of course, I could not go on without giving our kids, Isabelle and Matthew a shoutout for being my reason for living through the darkness.

AUTHOR'S NOTE

Please be aware that these are my own experiences, thoughts and beliefs.

If you were to ask other people in my life about what I detail in this book, they would have a different version to share.

That's because we all see the world differently, even when we walk side by side.

My hope is that by the end of this book, you will understand why that is.

Contents

DEDICATION iv

AUTHOR'S NOTE v

Contents vi

INTRODUCTION 1

WHAT IS A CHRONIC ILLNESS? 5

M.E./CFS SYMPTOMS 9

ABOUT THIS BOOK 11

HOW TO USE THIS BOOK 15

CHAPTER 1 18

You Are Destined For So Much More! 18

CHAPTER 2 24

Where It All Began 24

CHAPTER 3 38

What The F**k Is Happening To Me? 38

CHAPTER 4 47

It's Not Just My Story 47

    THE EGO MIND 52

        EXERCISE – THE TREE OF YOU 54

CHAPTER 5 56

Uncover Not Recover 56

CHAPTER 6 62

How I Saved Myself 62

CHAPTER 7 66

The Very Beginning 66

CHAPTER 8 72

The Specialist 72

CHAPTER 9	76
Neurologist	*76*
WHAT WOULD HAVE HELPED	83
CHAPTER 10	87
Nutritional Supplements	*87*
CHAPTER 11	92
Counselling	*92*
CHAPTER 12	101
The Nervous System	*101*
SYMPATHETIC NERVOUS SYSTEM (SNS)	105
PARASYMPATHETIC NERVOUS SYSTEM (PSNS)	107
AN IMBALANCED NERVOUS SYSTEM	111
TECHNIQUES FOR SOOTHING THE NERVOUS SYSTEM	112
CHAPTER 13	115
Trauma And The Nervous System	*115*
CHAPTER 14	122
Types Of Traumas	*122*
ACUTE TRAUMA	123
DEVELOPMENTAL TRAUMA	127
PRECONSCIOUS/PRECOGNITIVE TRAUMA	131
INTERGENERATIONAL TRAUMA	133
COLLECTIVE TRAUMA	135
CHAPTER 15	136
Trauma And Understanding Triggers	*136*
ANXIETY EXERCISE – THANK YOUR FUTURE SELF	144
EXERCISE TO USE WHEN YOU NOTICE YOURSELF BEING TRIGGERED	146
CHAPTER 16	150
Uncovering Trauma	*150*

CHAPTER 17 157
The Ups And Downs Of Living With M.E. 157
CHAPTER 18 164
A Shift In Mindset 164
CHAPTER 19 167
The Doctor Who ACTUALLY Listened 167
CHAPTER 20 169
The Mind 169
   MINDFULNESS 172
   BECOMING THE OBSERVER 175
   GRATITUDE 176
      GRATITUDE EXERCISES 179
   THE POWER OF THE MIND 183
CHAPTER 21 185
Yoga 185
      BREATHING EXERCISE 189
CHAPTER 22 190
Meditation 190
CHAPTER 23 197
Brainwaves 197
CHAPTER 24 202
Mitochondrial Therapy 202
CHAPTER 25 212
Awakening 212
CHAPTER 26 224
Sound Healing 224
   MY SOUND PRACTITIONER EXPERIENCE 227
CHAPTER 27 232

How Does Sound Healing Work? *232*

    CHAPTER 28 239

NLP *239*

    WHAT IS NLP, HOW DOES IT WORK? 241

    CHAPTER 29 244

NLP In Practice *244*

    MY NLP PRACTITIONER EXPERIENCE 248

        NLP EXERCISES 253

    CHAPTER 30 257

Inner Work Yoga Teacher Training *257*

    CHAPTER 31 267

The Themes Of Consciousness *267*

    CHAPTER 32 274

What Has All This Taught Me? *274*

    CHAPTER 33 279

What I Hope For You *279*

        EMOTIONAL ENQUIRY EXERCISE 281

    MY HOPES 282

    Recommended Reading 284

    Acknowledgements 285

    How to Work with Me 288

    References 289

INTRODUCTION

Well, who would have thought I'd write a book? Me, the girl who dropped her English AS level because writing an essay was so stressful, I cried my way through it – even though I achieved a B.

Why did it cause me so much stress? Because I didn't feel smart enough, intelligent enough or fancy enough. I could hardly remember what an adjective or verb were, and don't get me started on sentence structures.

Fast-forward sixteen years. I take the plunge to write, to share my story and everything I've learnt along this rollercoaster of a thing called 'life'.

It's funny, because it was right at the time of doing my AS levels that my life and my body began to change. At that time, I was a Welsh 800m athlete, training hard, achieving goals … but something was brewing beneath the surface. Sharp stabbing pains began and within eighteen months my body failed me. I was plagued with extreme fatigue, and training began to feel like I was running a marathon every day. My legs barely moving, pain searing through my muscles, exhaustion for hours, even days after. Something wasn't right!

What I loved doing most was gone, just like that.

A diagnosis, something I'd never heard of before: Myalgic Encephalomyelitis (M.E.) also referred to as chronic fatigue syndrome (CFS) (sometimes you will see it referred to as M.E./CFS, which is how I refer to it throughout this book). A chronic illness, an invisible illness, so many words to describe this one thing, yet no answers to heal from it, to understand it. Not even a test to truly diagnose it.

This book is the book I wished I had back then: something to explain what caused it, the effect of it, and the information and tools to be able to learn not just how to manage it but to begin to thrive again and potentially heal. This book is a guide, a guide back to hope, back to the light that may seem so far away or even invisible to you right now.

I spent years (and shit loads of money!) to learn about, to try to understand this illness; not just this illness but chronic illnesses in general. My thirst for knowledge gave me a thirst for life.

This led me to alternative therapies and treatments, opening myself up to a more spiritual, philosophical outlook on life. Like a door opening, possibilities found me and I went after each one that called to me.

That journey of trial and error, learning, failing, a dam full of tears, led me here, to you. To someone who knows this pain, who is still experiencing it, who craves something more, but just doesn't know where to start.

Journal entry – 4 November 2021

Today I am not OK! I haven't journaled for ages and I've been called to do it for weeks now but I'm just avoiding and making excuses.

I have decided to start writing a book. It was so liberating and exciting to finally decide to do it. However, it is unlocking so much that my body aches, I feel a lot of sadness coming out and so many tears. I'm feeling like I need to curl up in bed or just be hugged for hours on end.

Today it just hurts, like I want to scream and shout it all out. I feel so tired and yet all I want to do is write the book.

I know so deeply within my soul – my whole being in fact – that this book will help so many and I just want to help everyone right now. I also know it is a healing process for myself, hence these feelings. I just wasn't prepared for this. I hadn't considered that I'd physically feel this way, especially because I was so excited and liberated when I began.

I also feel like this is a test, a learning, to see if I really want to face all that I had hidden from, to see how much I really want to do this.

I don't want it to take years to do. I want to face it all and tackle it all so it doesn't have to hurt for long. To do that I need to create practices and set aside time to process and heal, otherwise it will swallow me whole!

And so that is how it all began. A deep knowing that this was needed, not just for myself but for others. To know you're not alone in your journey and that there is hope for you, even if it doesn't seem that way right now.

Start with me: let me share what I know, my own experiences, my own tools and techniques that I used to regain my life, my true identity. Know that there is something better for you, you just have to be open to learning, to trying, to failing, to hold yourself in compassion and love for who you were, who you are now and who you will be in the future.

WHAT IS A CHRONIC ILLNESS?

A chronic illness is a condition that lasts a year or more and requires ongoing medical attention and/or limits activities of daily living.[1]

What is M.E./CFS?

M.E. stands for Myalgic Encephalomyelitis – I know it's a mouthful, hence the abbreviated 'M.E.'. However, when you really look at the full meaning and begin to break it down, it gives you an accurate description of the illness.

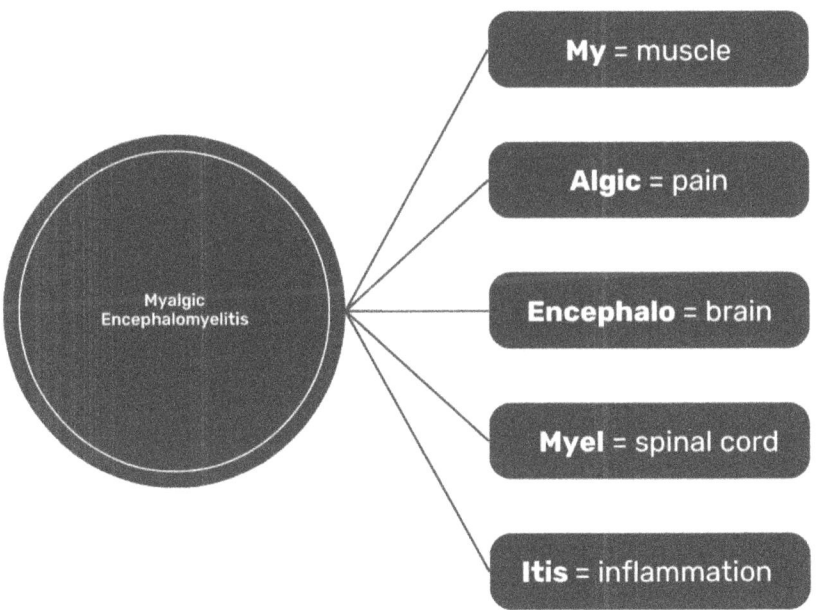

Figure 1. Explanation of Myalgic Encephalomyelitis

You can see that M.E. is literally referring to pain and inflammation of the muscles, brain and spinal cord. That's a lot, right? No, wonder the quality of life for sufferers drops so dramatically.

Let's take it a step further in connecting the dots. Your nervous system is made up of the brain and spinal cord. The spinal cord has nerves which then branch off and extend right through the body. So if you were to sum it all up to understand it simply: M.E. means your nervous system is not functioning at its optimal state, leading to symptoms. I'm going to expand on these symptoms a little further on.

I've explained what M.E./CFS means in its medical term, but what does it mean for those diagnosed with it? It is a complex, only partially understood multi-system disease with severity varying widely. I have been on both ends of this spectrum over the past fourteen years. Some days, weeks or even months the symptoms were mild, so I could go about my day normally – well, my version of normal. Then there were days, weeks, months and even years where they were moderate, meaning moving around took every ounce of energy from me. And then there were times when I had them severely, where I was housebound, wheelchair-bound, bed-bound, all the bounds that are not fun. When it was this severe, my words failed me, and even eating food became a challenge as it took too much energy to chew, let alone sit upright. Some people who live at the severe end of the spectrum are tube-fed and highly sensitive to light and sound.

Anyone can develop M.E./CFS, from children to older people. I have worked with thirteen-year-olds to sixty-year-olds. It more commonly develops during teenage and early adolescent years, but it is not exclusive to that age range. It is also found in twice as many women as men and affects any ethnicity.[2]

In the UK, M.E./CFS is thought to affect 250,000 people, and an estimated 836,000 to 2.5 million Americans, but about 90 per cent of people with M.E./CFS have not been diagnosed.[3,4] M.E./CFS affects every aspect of people's lives: to the point that 25 per cent of those 250,000 with a diagnosis have such severe symptoms that they are housebound or bed-bound. A study found that when M.E./CFS was compared with twenty different conditions – including stroke, rheumatoid arthritis, multiple sclerosis and some forms of cancer and schizophrenia – patients with M.E./CFS reported the lowest health-related quality of life.[5]

I have, however, noticed something in common with all the people I have spoken to and worked with: their illness stemmed from a trauma or a medical trigger (such as a virus) that they just never really recovered from (or both), leaving them in a perpetual state of illness. It was the same for me: an initial emotional trauma, paired with a virus a year later. I delve into the details of this later in the book.

It is an illness that affects so many parts of you. When you use the term 'body', most people only think of the physical body we can touch; we don't tend to think of the nervous system, the immune system, mitochondria or the digestive system. If you do, then you are many steps ahead of where I started.

It is all of these systems falling out of balance, becoming dysregulated that leads to the development of the catalogue of symptoms. However, it is my belief – due to my own experiences and experiences with my clients – that the true cause, the root cause of this happening in the first place is due to emotional trauma. A moment or phase in your life where you felt utterly rejected, abandoned, shamed: essentially, feeling unloved and unsafe affects the system, but at the time it goes unnoticed. Think of this emotional trauma as a wound that never healed; it was left to fester, leading to symptoms manifesting, which over time led to a chronic illness.

I now work as a trauma-informed holistic therapist, guiding chronic illness clients towards healing, using a combination of practices that guided me to my own recovery. I am a qualified reiki master, sound practitioner, certified NLP practitioner, and coach. I am also a spiritual mentor and sacred yoga and inner work teacher. Oh, and I like to draw and create things in my spare time, like oracle decks, tarot cards and silver jewellery. All the illustrations in this book are my own: the perfect combination of clarifying explanations for you and providing an outlet for my creativity.

This book explains what I have learnt about the cause and effect of trauma on your mind, body and spirit. It is a guide to help you peel back the layers of your illness, your symptoms and most of all to find the root cause of what created your chronic illness in the first place.

M.E./CFS SYMPTOMS

Symptoms vary widely and fluctuate greatly. Each person has their own experience, with symptoms and their severity looking very different from one sufferer to another. The list of symptoms truly can go on and on but here are the most common ones:

- Overwhelming fatigue
- Post-exertional malaise – worsening of symptoms after physical or mental activity that would not have caused a problem before illness
- Sleep disruptions – insomnia, unrefreshing sleep
- Cognitive impairment – brain fog, memory problems, poor concentration, difficulty retrieving or forming words
- Painful muscles and joints
- Stress-related symptoms – anxiety, panic, difficulty tolerating stress
- Headaches – of a new type, pattern or severity
- Nausea
- Heart palpitations
- Sensory overload – lights becoming too bright and sounds feeling like a jackhammer in your head
- Immune symptoms – tender lymph nodes, recurrent sore throats, fevers or flu-like symptoms, and new food or chemical sensitivities

- Orthostatic intolerance – symptoms become worse when standing; can be diagnosed as postural tachycardia syndrome (PoTS)
- Gastrointestinal issues – bloating, indigestion, gas, diarrhoea or constipation

I had every one of these symptoms, but you do not need to have them all to be diagnosed. For me, it started with one, then over time this grew to experiencing them all. The final symptoms I developed were tremors and muscle spasms, but they are not on the list as they're not that common.

ABOUT THIS BOOK

I truly believe everything happens for a reason and even though I've had the idea of writing a book years ago, I knew I wasn't ready to unpack my life until now. It wouldn't have been as powerful as I believe it has now become, because I hadn't learnt all I needed to know until now.

I first started writing a book five or six years ago, but I knew I wasn't ready. I didn't have my life back. Not in the way I do now. Back then, I felt like a fraud writing a book as I was still poorly, still suffering with symptoms and I was worried that I could get worse, plagued with thoughts of *Who do you think you are writing about a better life when you still suffer so badly at times? How can you help anyone if you can't fix yourself?*

Now, however, I have been symptom-free for four years and I am finally giving myself permission to share my story, detailing the tools and techniques I learnt along the way and that I still use to this day.

It hasn't been an easy journey, which you will see. I would think that I'd recovered, only to find my symptoms would return (admittedly, never as badly as before). It took me years and many ups and downs to get to this point. It's also funny because I never once set out to find a cure, to heal myself; it was more about finding a way to be a better mum to my kids. I was just looking for a way to create more energy. Sounds good, you might think. But saying that I would never cure or heal myself limited any sort of possibility of achieving just that. I probably could have become symptom-free sooner if it wasn't for my unconscious and its self-sabotaging programs. Because, you see it was so engrained into me that there was no getting better that I would unconsciously prove that part of myself right by having a flare-up. Keeping me stuck – or as my mind perceived it, keeping me safe! I expand on this in great detail throughout the book, but it's something I wish I'd known as soon as I'd received my diagnosis, or even just as a child, which is why I'm making you aware of it now.

You will find that the timeline can jump around quite a lot during the peak of my worst physical and mental symptoms, due to it being so difficult to recall – classic trauma sign.

This book is a guide. It is a form of education for those who also find themselves lost, unsure of who they are; those who are looking for more out of life, a better quality of life.

This is my way to reach more people and bring as much healing as I possibly can to as many people as I possibly can. The fact that you are actually holding this book in your hands right now is completely mind-blowing and ridiculously exciting to me. My hope is that you find acceptance, love, peace and an understanding for yourself – and maybe even for those around you, too.

I truly believe that everyone should be taught all that I've learnt about the effect the mind has on the body and vice versa. It should be taught to everyone from birth, because if we did that, we would all have a much better understanding of who we truly are at our soul level, instead of who we currently believe ourselves to be, which is a version of yourself you've created to please others and blend into society so you can feel accepted. The truth is, acceptance doesn't come from outside of yourself, it comes from within, and this is what you will learn throughout this book.

They say knowledge is power and that used to trigger me, as I used to associate the word 'power' with being something bad, something that means *I'm better than you*, or used to control others. However, rather than using power in the sense of control, I now see how power comes from within. The knowledge I have to empower myself can also empower others! It wasn't a conscious decision to reframe the word 'power' but I naturally came to see a new meaning around the word, which progressed to focusing on empowerment.

I feel so strongly about sharing how interconnected the mind, body and spirit are; and also how our lives are not set in stone. No matter how awful it may be right now, you can change it. As I write this, I know it triggers a few people with thoughts like *There's nothing I can do ... This is it for me ... Here we go again, another book telling me it's all in my head.* I promise you that I 100 per cent understand that. *How?* you may ask. Because I was you. I would roll my eyes at a suggestion of a self-help book or someone saying it's just about thinking positive, it will get better blah, blah, blah. And now look at me writing these same words! Truly impressive when you think about it because it was only four years ago that I still truly believed I would never be symptom-free.

The secret you need to know is who you currently think you are right now is not actually true! I know that is a bit confusing. It's exactly what I thought when someone told me this. I learnt it was because my mind literally couldn't understand this concept: it was not what I was taught growing up, it wasn't what I saw in society so how could this be true?

When I talk about the mind, I'm not referring to the way some doctors and health professionals dismissively say, "It's all in your head, you're over-exaggerating," essentially gaslighting you. I've had this exact experience, which I discuss later in the book. I know that what you are feeling and the symptoms you are experiencing are VERY real, and I will never tell you otherwise. When I talk about the mind, I mean the unconscious – the deeper layers we are not aware are playing out, which can go right back to childhood.

On my journey, I began to peel back a layer at a time to uncover this meaning, albeit by accident most of the time. Now I know, however, it wasn't an accident at all. Everything fell into place exactly as it needed to, even though most of the time I had no idea what the fuck was going on. I believe you picked this book up for a reason and I hope that you find compassion for yourself, a knowing that you are not alone in what you are experiencing. I hope you create a belief that there is more for you and that your hope begins to burn brightly.

HOW TO USE THIS BOOK

I want this book to be a book that you want to finish and *can* finish. I cannot tell you how many non-fiction, self-help books I have that I've never finished or just never opened. So I decided to write my book as a book that tells a story. A story of my life and journey, in my voice, so (as I'm sure you've figured out already) there will be swearing along the way as well as my raw and honest realisations.

I've also divided the book into short chapters as I know how difficult it can be to concentrate for long periods of time when you have brain fog and chronic fatigue. You may want to read one chapter per day. This may help with absorbing the information I share, as well as being less overwhelming if you're experiencing brain fog. It is also a great way to create a new positive habit for yourself. Nuggets of knowledge are woven throughout the book alongside (short!) chapters which broaden your understanding of pivotal concepts, but all in plain English. And I don't bombard you with a whole section of science, studies etc. You're welcome.

You will find the section on trauma is comprehensive and that is because it is crucial to your potential to heal. It doesn't matter if you don't understand it as you read it right now. You can come back to it as many times as you want. I'll bet the second time you read it, it'll make more sense as the information clicks into place after reading the whole book.

As you go through the book you will find I've added exercises that are the exact ones I used for myself and that I also use with my clients. All the exercises can be found on my website via www.hope-light.co.uk/bookresources, so if you want to hear my glorious voice talking you through them, you can. You will also find some extra goodies there too.

It's crucial that you read this book in order. It wasn't as simple as just deciding to get better then going to one session of a particular therapy that healed me. It was a physical and emotional battle and I want you to feel that battle, all the setbacks, all the highs and lows, and I want you to grasp the incremental changes which build throughout each chapter, until I reached the point of when I DID heal.

Why do I want you to feel this? Because I know that you know my battle, in your own story. I want you to get to the end of this book and truly believe you, too, can have a better quality of life.

My editor said this truly beautiful thing that I felt summed the journey of this book up, 'You started with hope and ended with light' and she couldn't be any more accurate if she tried. I would have gained so much (maybe even healed sooner) if someone had given me or allowed me to hope, but an M.E. diagnosis rips that from you as medical professionals wash their hands of you as to them there is no hope! But that is not true, so that's what I'm doing now: I'm providing hope, giving you permission to hope. 'Don't underestimate the power of hope. I would never have reached the light without the hope that sparked it.'[6]

I need to add that this book is not for self-diagnosing. It is not a 'cure all'. You should always seek professional advice if you are concerned about any symptoms.

I just hope that this book will awaken your hope, and teach you tools and techniques that you can use in the real world and gain a better quality of life.

However, if you are looking for a quick fix, then this book is not for you.

CHAPTER 1

You Are Destined For So Much More!

I never really considered myself as ever hitting rock bottom. I couldn't have, I hadn't been through as much shit as others have been through. I'd not lost many loved ones, I've not been homeless, or abused. I used to always brush things off and say *It could be worse.* I would think about all the people in the world going through so much more than I was and that I should count myself lucky that what I have experienced is it. Every time I felt sorry for myself, I'd instantly hear that thought in my mind, *Don't be so dramatic, it could be so much worse!*

Over time I came to realise that this isn't true. It really doesn't matter whether people are going through or have been through worse than you; you are still going through what you are going through. Your pain is your pain, your grief is your grief, and that constant negative mental chatter is yours! You are experiencing it all. Giving myself permission to feel sorry for myself was one of the most powerful things I could do: it allowed me to feel again, which allowed me to process.

This let me see things differently and as I went on my healing journey, I realised I did in fact have a 'rock bottom', my turning moment, my moment of awakening. I still remember that moment like it was yesterday. It's always stuck with me and reappeared every time I've felt myself slipping.

I was twenty-four, living in a massive three-storey house, with beige tall walls, which made me feel so small. This huge, quiet and empty house ... empty, this is how I felt inside. The kids were in school, and my husband was at work. I was once again lying on the sofa with Walter the wheelchair tucked up tight against the sofa to my right, ready at all times to support me in my quest to not pee myself. The TV was on, playing yet another film in an attempt to haul me away from my reality. My mind chaotic with thoughts like *I'm done ... I can't keep going on like this ... I'm so exhausted ... I can't take much more, it isn't fair!* amongst the cries of despair and chronic pains that plagued my body.

You'd think that would be enough torture to endure but no, it didn't stop there. I lay in utter fear, scared that if I moved even just a teeny, tiny bit I would set off the full-body tremors and muscle spasms that had been afflicting me, and they were so fucking exhausting! I had been living with them for the past ten months now and they were relentless. They have no mercy, they do not care that I'm a shell of a person, that I'm getting thinner and thinner, that my body is full of lactic acid, barely able to create new energy or absorb oxygen for my body to even survive. I had no control over them, there were no warning signs. I could be walking fine one moment and then be on the floor in full-on 'body attack'. There were times when I actually looked like I was having an epileptic fit but I was fully conscious and aware of what was going on around me. Sometimes I wished I wasn't aware, that I could have just blacked out and escaped, just for a moment of peace.

I was lying on this sofa crying and crying and crying some more between the lulls in the films or once it finished, as that was when I came back to my reality, back to my pain, back to the shambles that was my life.

The cries got so aggressive sometimes too, you know when you're almost screaming because you literally don't know what else to do with all the anger and frustration brewing inside? I wanted to throw things, oh how I dreamed and imagined myself throwing things. However, I couldn't in case it set the tremors off, and my god I would be so pissed off with myself if I had done that. Not to mention that I'd also have had to clear it all up before anyone came home because god forbid anyone found out I wasn't coping, that I needed help or that some days I wanted to check out of this world altogether and just be done with it. I was just so exhausted mentally, physically, emotionally. I don't even know where my spirit up and went off to, but it sure as hell wasn't here.

As much as I wanted to be done with this world at times, I also didn't want to leave. The love I had for those around me was too strong, thankfully. I couldn't leave them with the aftermath of that action. I will be forever grateful for my mind presenting me with an image of someone having to find me and what those around me would have to endure.

My first thought was, *Who would find me?* I imagined the trauma that it would cause them for the rest of their lives, the guilt that would ensue and the unanswered questions or what ifs. One of my first thoughts was, *Man, the kids would be so screwed up, Lee (my husband) is as emotional as a brick wall and the kids would never feel their feelings or talk about anything then, they'd lock that shit up so tight and that could lead to such destructive behaviour and so much more as they grow up,* so I thank Lee so much for being an emotional brick wall because if he wasn't I might not be here right now. (Although one brick from his wall has come down since, he still seems to be allergic to the word 'feel').

Back to my moment on the sofa. Lying there with all this chaos running through my mind, I remember thinking, *This is it, I've had my life.* I'd got to experience such joy and pride as an athlete, which I'd been successful at. I didn't reach my goal of the Olympics but I did have so much fun trying. I'd met the love of my life and had two incredible children, *How lucky am I to have been able to have experienced so much love? I've experienced more than most of my friends in such a short time, maybe that's my lot. Now all I can do is be here and watch them from the shadows.*

I remember an image of my kids coming to my mind at that moment, an image of them playing together, their little faces smiling and laughing like they were right there but I couldn't reach them; it was as if they were in a different world to me. Their world colourful, bright, energetic, happy and full of laughter, and mine dark, cold, twisted, lost and full of utter despair. It's funny because, obviously, this was in my mind yet it felt like they were right there, just to the right of me in the corner of the room, like there was a portal in my house to this awesome, joyful place where they were playing. I can even see the green T-shirt and red shorts Matthew was wearing and the floral dress Isabelle had on. The imagery was so detailed and there was this beautiful golden sun energy surrounding them as they ran around playing tag. I could hear this outpour of laughter as Matthew tagged Isabelle. It was so infectious; it brought a smile to my face and tears ran down my cheeks.

21

I wanted to join them, I felt myself reaching out to them … Figuratively of course, as I was way too scared to move and it would have been a waste of energy that I could have used to drink my water, plus it was all in my head so I'd literally have been reaching for nothing and, knowing my luck, would have fallen off the sofa, landing head first, setting off my tremors and then have to lie there for a few hours until my body had settled and I could get myself back up to the sofa, which would set off the tremors again … and around and around I'd go.

I turned my head to glance back at the TV, back to reality, feeling utterly broken and wanting it all to end while simultaneously feeling ridiculously guilty for thinking such a thing and how selfish I was to even consider it, but I was just so exhausted I didn't know how to get through yet another day. It was like my soul was screaming out, praying for it all to be over. It was then at that moment that I heard, *You are destined for so much more than this.* I know, I know: *What do you mean, you heard? Was there someone else in the room with you?* I mean it was my own voice in my head but at the same time, it wasn't coming from inside my head: it came from the end of the sofa, slightly to the right as if someone was standing there, and yet there was no one there.

It's a hard one to describe, but have you ever had that feeling that someone is watching you or had an experience where you could have sworn someone was right behind you only to turn around and no one was there? It was like that. The voice was so calm and so clear. It was like a sudden silence amongst the chaos, a sense of peace, a relief. And oh my, the feeling that washed over me, it was so comforting and reassuring and it resonated so deeply within me, I felt it in every cell of my being, like it touched my soul. I just believed it wholeheartedly; there was no doubt in my mind that it was true.

When I recall the memory in my mind it's like a polaroid picture, where most of the image is in the dark, with a smoky wash over it, where you can just make out the sofa through the smoke. Then there is this one spot that is in colour, a golden light, where I could spot someone's presence: that is where I heard the voice coming from. It was like a glimmer of hope, a light.

This was the moment I decided to live!

CHAPTER 2

Where It All Began

The cause

There once was a big bang and from that ... jokes ... fast-forward a few billion years to a hospital in a small town called Rinteln in Germany on 1 October 1989, where at 12:07pm a beautiful baby girl was born. I say 'beautiful' but at over 9 lb, it may be questionable. Yes, that's right, it was me, a mini sumo wrestler. Named Katie Rose: Katie means 'pure' and Rose, well that's self-explanatory. You now have all the information you need to check out my birth chart or human design, meaning we can now call each other friends. So welcome to my world, friend, and as we are now friends, I feel I can share my story with you.

My childhood growing up was a pretty normal and standard one. I remember being outside a lot, laughing, having fun and going on little adventures, whether that was by myself, with my brother or on holidays with my family. I always felt I was extremely lucky with what I had and that I had both parents who loved me and I loved them.

My dad was in the army so we moved around a lot, which I hated. Making new friends, trying to figure out where I fitted in only to leave them in a few months or a couple of years. That's why I was thrilled when, in 1999, I found out we were making our final move to Wales. However, I was not prepared for the new language and I always felt just 'less than', or even stupid as I didn't understand my school work, conversations or jokes in my new school. I can pretty much understand it now but only if someone isn't talking too fast and I have the mental energy to concentrate on the words to then translate to English. I still find it awkward when there's a word or two that I don't know, because while I'm trying to figure out what that word could be I end up losing the rest of the conversation, and well, by then I just feel like a right idiot. It's why I always say 'Sorry, I don't speak Welsh' or I'll answer in English.

Despite the language barrier, the new house was amazing: it was a few miles from the main road, down a country lane. It was run-down but my parents were doing it up bit by bit. I didn't care though as I spent most of the time outside, we had our own woods down the back of the house and my brother and I would spend our days exploring them. The woods were so steep that we would have to pick a tree to aim for so we could grab it in an attempt to stop ourselves from falling, or at least slow ourselves down.

We used to take ration packs and we would pretend to be soldiers or survivalists with our tree stump seats and a very see-through den. Made from tree branches and string, it actually looked more like a fort as we didn't have a roof. It was also massive; we could have had about eight people in there with us.

We would ride our bikes to go meet our friends and completely disappear for the day, only going home when we were hungry. I always remember it as being so freeing and fun. As a mum now I don't know how my parents let us disappear for the day with no way to communicate with us. We didn't have mobile phones back then and when we did get them there was no bloody signal anyway and you'd have to find that one perfect spot in the window to be able to get a text message out.

We made friends with the kids down the road. One day, when I was about ten, I was playing at their house and the girl was going to a running club that night and her mum said she'd take me too if I wanted to go, so I did. I'd always loved running and sports days, so I figured why not? It turned out I absolutely loved it. I went every week after that and I started doing fun runs and cross-country races. I surprised myself at how well I did, it was so infectious and my mum did the fun runs too – she had always been a runner and has done the London marathon three times. I loved doing something I was good at, it was completely uplifting and freeing.

In time I gave athletics a go and quickly realised I preferred it, with my absolute favourite race being the 800m. I also preferred running in the sunny weather not getting covered in mud, though I still did cross-country as part of my winter training for the summer. I began to train for the 800m and became pretty bloody good at it, representing West Wales and then Wales. I would race nearly every weekend throughout the year. I made some amazing friends and I just felt like I was living my best life. This was where I truly felt like I could be myself and it was OK to shine here, not by saying I was good but by allowing the races to say it for me. I cannot tell you the giddy feeling I got when I heard another athlete walk past whispering 'Oh no, Katie Parkes is here.' It gave me such an ego boost.

I represented Wales many times in both cross-country and athletics. I trained six times a week, travelling two hours, once a week to train with my coach and other athletes. I went warm weather training to Portugal two or three times, too. My parents took me to races nearly every weekend, which included lots of races outside of Wales. They supported me with it all. By 2003 I was one of the best 800m athletes in Wales, winning the Welsh Championships and School Championships a few times.

Life was great, right? I had supportive parents who went all around the country with me, I had a beautiful country home and I had great friends.

Obviously, something went wrong because well, why the hell would I be writing a book on hope and recovery from a chronic illness otherwise. At the age of fifteen, everything I knew and believed to be true was about to start falling apart.

I'd like to take a moment to reiterate the author's note here (in case you skipped it). From this point on, it's very much my perception, feelings, beliefs, and memories. Everyone in my life at this time will have different versions of events. That doesn't mean I'm wrong, or even that they're wrong. All versions are true, as they reflect the truth of the individual based on their own past experiences, beliefs, perceptions, and how they process and regulate their own emotions. I can only share my version of events.

I had gone to running club like I did every Thursday night and I saw my dad talking to one of my friend's mums. They looked like they were having such a serious conversation and I remember turning to my friend and asking what they were talking about, because it looked intense! I told her to be sure to tell me if she found out. We giggled and carried on being the awesome teenagers that we were.

I jumped in the car ready to go home but my dad didn't start the car, there was just silence. I can still remember where the car was parked: up by the school on the gravel car park facing the school wall.

It was getting darker and I can't remember if anything was said before what came next, I just remember my dad saying 'I have to tell you something ...' followed by a pause. Then he said, 'Your mum and I are going to be getting a divorce.'

Now here's the weirdest part, I felt so relaxed at that moment and I remember feeling like it was a relief, like something washed over me in that moment. It had always confused me as to why I felt like that because I had a good childhood, it wasn't like I lived in chaos, with screaming and shouting all the time. My parents never really argued in front of us, so there was no reason as to why I felt such relief in that moment. Growing up, I must have had a sense that my parents weren't happy.

That wasn't it though, he wasn't finished yet. This is the part that hit me hard, that was so unexpected, that I was not prepared for at all. He said, 'So I'll be moving to a different country.' Now that threw me, that caught me off guard; I was utterly confused. I responded with a 'HUH, DIFFERENT COUNTRY?!' turning my head to look at him with such force my ponytail flipped forwards at high speed from the sheer force of the whip, and then my own momentum propelled me backwards in my seat. Well, at least that is how it is stored in my mind, it was probably a lot less dramatic than that but in that moment I suddenly understood the phrase 'taken aback' as I literally felt myself do it. He replied, 'There's another woman involved' and told me he would be moving to be with her. That is the last moment I remember. I don't know if I said any more or just fell silent. I have a feeling I just withdrew, feeling smaller and smaller in that grey fabric passenger seat.

The next bit I remember is walking up the stairs, but not walking from the bottom of the stairs, it was like I came back into my body as I was nearly at the top of the stairs, walking to my bedroom. I sat down on my purple futon and started doing my homework. I also couldn't tell you if my mum came to check on me or not, it's just a blank hole.

Everything from this moment on is a blur: the timeline of things is muddled up or there are complete gaps. As you can imagine, writing this book became extremely difficult at times because of this, but if you're ready, then come and step into my blurry world with me. From that day, everything changed. Not because my dad left and went to live with the other woman but because he didn't! ... I know, plot twist, right?! I was told about the divorce and the affair but then nothing! It was never spoken about again to me! Well, at least not that I can recall anyway. It was almost as if it had never happened, yet I knew it had because of the fallout that was happening all around me. I felt like I was invisible, like I didn't exist. Neither my mum nor dad sat down with me to check in, to see how I was doing, to talk about things that were happening in the house. There may have been one time as I vaguely remember sitting on the sofa, perhaps with Mum, but I couldn't tell you if it was to do with this or if I was getting told off for something – like I said the timeline becomes all muddled. I do know no one talked about what was happening in the house at the time or in the future. I also don't think I could have even expressed what was really going on inside my mind as I didn't have the words to describe the pain, hurt, betrayal and anger. I was never taught how to express negative feelings, or any overwhelming feelings in general, I would just end up crying every time I tried, even if it was good news. It was like there were no processing filters and it all became too much for my body, so out came all the tears.

The image that comes to mind when thinking back to that time is of a black and white movie of me as a little girl (not a teenager, interestingly enough) sitting at the top of the stairs as chaos ensues around me like a tornado, the whole house being ripped apart by the pain, hurt, screams and words being used like daggers all around me. It's as if the roof is caving in, yet she sits in complete silence, as if she is in the eye of the storm. I know, it's movie-worthy imagery.

It wasn't until about ten years later, when I started to speak to my mum about these events, that I discovered just how much of that time was in fact directly connected to the chronic illness I ended up living with. I've not really sat and had a conversation with my dad about it all as I was unsure whether to say something or not, worried I'd offend him or he'd try to shut me down and change the subject - that's just how he copes with things. So for years there were just no conversations about any of it.

Trying to recall this time of my life is like peeling through a layer of candy floss. I regularly dissociated, which I know now was a way of coping – a form of protection. As far as I remember I just went about my days as normal, though I recall a few times in school when I broke down or just randomly started crying for no reason, at the time unable to understand why. From the outside I must have seemed like a right attention-seeker because when anyone asked what was wrong all I could reply with was 'I don't know' because at that time I really didn't know, I didn't have words to express it and my mind couldn't comprehend it all. Now I know my unconscious mind was screaming for help, but I was missing the emotional knowledge to vocalise it.

It got worse in the house; the aftermath of finding out about the affair followed by my dad staying was awful. When I look back at it now I can see it wasn't the affair itself that got to me, it was the years of lying and the hypocrisy of it all that hurt the most. My dad was so tough on us when it came to morality, making it clear what was right and what was wrong, and the fear he instilled in us for doing anything wrong, well it was not worth the lie.

The woman involved in the affair would call the house phone and I just remember my heart breaking for my mum as she tried to keep it all together, but this woman just wouldn't stop ringing, wanting to talk to my dad and then wanting to talk to my mum and ugh, it was so painful to listen to. We actually had to change our house number in the end.

I honestly don't know how my mum made it through all that. She would try to just let the phone ring out but this woman must have just kept pressing the fucking redial button. I knew about the phone calls because I would sit at the top of the stairs and listen, although I could have just stayed in my room and heard it all from there because my room was directly above where the phone was plugged in, plus it wasn't like they were being quiet. I have a feeling my mum had told me not to answer the phone, but again it's a blur. I just sat in the middle of all this chaos, like I wasn't even there, like what was going on wouldn't affect me too. My brother wasn't living at home at this point, so I was going through it all on my own. Hearing the pain, the hurt, the anger and despair in my mum's voice as she tried so hard to tell this woman to go away and leave her alone. The woman couldn't accept that dad wasn't moving to be with her.

Instead, he moved into a caravan a hundred metres down the road. I honestly think it would have been so much easier for me and mum if he had moved to be with her, or at least further away than a hundred fucking metres. He also worked from our garage making wooden gates, so I had to see him every day. It was like I was supposed to carry on as if nothing had happened. This! This was when I started to feel the anger stirring within me. Always having to see him, after everything he had put us through, with no real apology.

Growing up it was drilled into us time and time again about how important rules were. You do as you're told, ALWAYS! Don't break the law or you will go to jail ... OK, I know that one is obvious but it was the *fear* that was drilled into us that if we did something bad, bad things will happen. If we took one step out of line there would be consequences. If we did anything wrong and lied about it, oh my it was horrible, there would be a lot of shouting and when my dad shouts, my god do you feel the vibrations through your entire body, it used to scare the shit out of me. It was as if my whole body would go on alert, I'm honestly surprised I didn't pee myself sometimes. I stood frozen, scared to move or say anything in case I said something wrong.

The worst for me was sitting at the dinner table: I would eat with my knife in my left hand and my fork in my right, which apparently is the incorrect way to eat and my dad would remind me of this every time – you'd think I was training to be a fucking princess or something with how angry he would get about it. He would shout and make me switch them back. It was utterly terrifying, the way he used to shout. I'd look at my mum for help, for safety, but she rarely said anything. On the few occasions she did, she would be shut down too. I was left feeling hurt, powerless, and alone. The number of times I would sit crying at that dinner table is quite ridiculous. All I wanted to do in those moments was run away and hide. I wanted to protect myself. I didn't want to eat after that because I couldn't stop sobbing, but I wasn't allowed to leave the table until everyone had finished, so I'd sit there crying into my food, trying to eat between the sobs.

I would just like to point out that this book is not about attacking my dad, I love him very much and I have so many great memories and times with him, even to this day. We now know he was suffering from PTSD at the time, and looking back it really does explain a lot. And after everything I have now learnt I fully understand how he came to make the decisions that led to specific actions and behaviours. However, I feel it is important to share these things and how I felt at the time (as a child, without the emotional knowledge I now have as an adult – plus a few life experiences under the belt) because it all relates to further on down the line when I discovered the root causes of the chronic illness that developed, which I'll explain later in the book. In the end, it all boils down to trauma, and every trauma is emotional, whether it's 'big' like an affair or seemingly 'small' like eating without royal grace.

One morning as I was walking down the stairs, I could see the pull-out sofa was out. The lower I got down the stairs, the faster my heart rate became – my stomach dropped, as if I already knew. I reached the bottom of the stairs and there he was, sleeping on the sofa. I remember this feeling in the pit of my stomach and pure confusion in my mind. No one had told me he was going to be there. The next thing I remember is him living with us again. Again, no conversation; just one big happy family. I don't know if there was a discussion once I was downstairs or not. I just know in that moment I felt confused and hurt.

The craziest part about all of this is we literally did go about our days like it was all completely normal! – There's nothing quite like a denial coping mechanism, sweeping it all under the rug.

As time went on I really started to spiral. Again, I can't say at which point this began but basically, I became a pro at having conversations with my mum and my dad in my mind. If no one was going to talk to me in 'real life' I would make them have conversations in my head. I would scream and shout and say everything I wanted to say, they would reply, and then I'd scream and shout some more. This was going on in a loop in my mind, every single day, with the majority happening at night. As soon as I got into bed it was like the gates opened and the same conversations would begin: *How dare you? Who do you think you are coming back into our lives like nothing happened? How am I supposed to just pretend that everything is normal? What are you thinking, Mum?* I also found myself wishing I was ill, thinking, *If I had cancer then they would have to see me, I wouldn't be invisible any more, they would love me again,* because at the core of it all I felt unlovable and abandoned, that no one cared about me, and I was supposed to be a good little girl and do what they expected of me even though it went against everything that I was feeling.

I tried journaling all this shit out, all this hurt, pain, anger, rage and loneliness as I saw an article in a teen magazine saying it was a great outlet. But it just made me even angrier and I was so worried my parents would find my journal that I would hide it. I felt so ashamed of all the things I'd written. I buried a few in the bin, under all the stuff that was already in there and I even burnt one. I found a hiding place for my journal in the end. I would remove the bottom drawer in my bedside table and put my journal on the floor, then I'd put the drawer back in and boom! A dark hole for my dark thoughts. In time, a bottle of vodka would keep me and my journal company in those moments of *AAAHHHH, FUCK YOU, FUCK THE WORLD, I HATE YOU ALL!!!!!* Later on, a razor blade would join the black hole too. This one is the hardest one for me to admit to because I still hold so much shame around it. At the time I just felt I no longer had any control and I had no say in anything, and this was the only way I could gain back some control. I cut myself a few times on my hip, never very deep. I just wanted to feel like I could make one choice for myself. I found relief in that moment while listening to Britney Spears's song 'Everytime' on repeat. This song spoke to me in so many ways and as I look back at the lyrics now I see how they were another representation of how desperate I was for help.

    I remember a battle going on in my mind at this time when I started cutting, thinking, *This will give me control and make me feel better,* along with, *You know this will not help or change anything.* I felt so ashamed that I did it because I really did know deep down that it wasn't going to change anything. After about a few weeks, maybe a month, I stopped. I thought, *That was fucking stupid and pointless,* like I had suddenly woken up.

    As the months went by, all this anger just kept building, more and more. It was like a virus in my mind, it completely took over. I started raiding my parents' alcohol cupboard to quieten my mind, which I did more and more frequently until I drank so much one night I passed out and threw up everywhere. I don't recall any of this, however, and in all honesty, I do not want to as I cringe at the thought of it and my heart rate increases as I write this knowing my parents (I think it was my dad) found me in that state. I'm pretty sure he did try talking to me at this time but by this point, I had so much anger and hatred towards him I didn't want to speak to him or even be around him. I wanted to punch him, hit him, scream at him and tell him to get out of my life, which is completely heart-breaking now because if I knew then what I know now, I wouldn't have had to be stuck in such hatred and I could have regulated my emotions and understood where they were really coming from and why. However, I just couldn't get my head around how he could do what he did, only to then stay and pretend nothing happened.

I considered running away at this point, to hide at a friend's house until it was all over but I was so worried it would get me into trouble or cause my mum even more pain I decided not to. I had also written numerous letters to my mum with all my thoughts; my anger. But I ripped them all up into tiny pieces and put them in the bin. I just couldn't bring myself to do it, until one day I came up with a plan. I decided I'd leave the letter outside her bedroom door while my dad took me for my hair appointment or something, so I knew only Mum would be able to find it. When I got home the sheer terror set in and I ran up those stairs faster than Usain Bolt, only to find an empty space outside her bedroom door. My heart rate spiked, I felt sick, I didn't know what to do and I don't remember what I actually did; all I remember next is my mum coming into my room to say she'd read the letter. The panic running through my body at that moment was so intense, I was so scared and unsure what was going to happen, *Would she hate me? Would she tell Dad? What was going to happen to me?* She sat down beside me, wrapped her arm around me, pulled me in close to her and said, 'I'm so sorry.' I know she said more than that but I can't remember, as I was bawling my eyes out.

It felt like the next day my dad left, though it might have been days or weeks later. I just felt such a relief and like I didn't have to hide or pretend any more. I believe I was nearly eighteen at this point.

CHAPTER 3

What The F**k Is Happening To Me?

The effect

A few months after I found out about the affair, I had glandular fever. It was GCSE year, so I would have been sixteen. I had to take a week off school, and I obviously had to stop training. Taking time off from training was the absolute worst. Running was where I would escape: that was my world, my place of safety. I remember feeling so shit, my entire body felt like it couldn't move, like I'd been hit by a lorry. I just remember being on the sofa constantly, barely moving. I was so fatigued, I felt so sick, and my brain felt so slow, like it wasn't able to process information. I spent days on the sofa watching film after film after film, trying to escape into someone else's life or a fantasy world, somewhere, anywhere that took my mind away from my body.

I went back to training not long after going back to school, I probably should have had more time off school and training but being in school meant I didn't have to be at home. The training started with short runs at home; I had to build back up so slowly. At this point, my body felt more like it had been run over by a motorbike rather than a lorry, so I decided that was good enough to get back to training. I am very aware now that my body was not ready for this at all but all I knew then was I needed my world back.

The next two years were an absolute battle. I eventually got back to my daily training programme and my mum would take me to

Cardiff (a two-hour drive) once a week so I could train with my coach and other athletes. I fought so hard to get back to where I was before having glandular fever, I put everything I had into my training and I cannot tell you the pure joy and liberation I felt when I hit my first PB (personal best) after the virus. Then out of nowhere I crashed, I got a cold or something and my training went to shit. I managed to get back to feeling good again, training my ass off and then I crashed again: it went on like this for the next two years. It got harder and harder to climb back but each time I'd eventually hit those PBs and it all felt worth it.

Why did I keep getting back up to try again and again? Because I loved it, I loved working to be the best. I had a dream of reaching the Olympics, ever since my nan (my mum's mum, Mrs Morna May Dallyn) turned to me one day while we sat in her kitchen watching the Olympics on a small square box TV (sitting on a wooden bench with one of those thin foam cushions that if you sat there too long you'd get a numb bum) and said, 'I'll be watching you there one day.' I remember my reply was a giggle but internally I remember suddenly feeling like it was possible for me to achieve it; from that moment on it was my dream. I finally had this belief in myself. I had struggled to find that for myself before, I finally felt like I was good enough.

At seventeen, I started getting these excruciating pains in my head, so sharp and painful, they were utterly crippling at times. It was like someone had a big-ass kitchen knife and had plunged it into my head, then pulled it out. Just like that the pain would stop for a few seconds only for the knife to be plunged back in. Sometimes it was like that imaginary fucker holding the knife would wiggle it around just to see what would happen.

The first time I experienced it was while I was revising for my AS levels. I was sitting at the table in our front room while my mum laid laminate flooring (she is a chronic DIYer). I remember it because I'd never experienced pain like that. The first few weren't excruciating, but I definitely knew they were there. I found it hard to concentrate and focus on revising; each day or week the intensity just got worse and worse.

I went to the doctor's. I loved my doctor at the time, Dr Roberts: he was always so kind and patient with me. I'd always walk in, sit down, and he'd ask how I was and I'd reply 'fine,' and he'd just smile. Then one day he looked at me and said, 'If you were fine I don't think you'd be in my office.' I remember thinking, *Wow, that is so true, why did I say that?* It was the need to please others, to not be a burden. Anyway, at this appointment for my headaches he gave me some tablets for the pains but nothing seemed to help at all and I was now starting to get so tired all the time. I would be in the sixth-form room with my friends and all I wanted to do was sleep. Even moving to go to class felt challenging, as if my body was a dead weight.

My training started to feel harder and harder over the next few months, even though my training programme hadn't changed. There was a fear brewing inside me as I couldn't understand what was going on. I was feeling so exhausted all the time. I had started 'spinning' around town in my red Corsa, named 'Chutterbug' as it would chut, chut, chutter its way up steep hills. I remember being at a friend's house and falling asleep in the middle of the day, waking up thinking, *That was so weird*. I figured it was from the stress of doing my A-level exams as I had not long finished them.

On 8 June 2008, I drove myself to a race. I was so tense and anxious about driving there as it was the furthest I'd driven on my own. I wasn't used to driving on busy roads, I lived in the country, where there's really not that much traffic. I parked up and found out my race would be starting in just thirty minutes, which I had not expected at all. I found my club, dropped my bags and began my warm-up. I started the 800m race, feeling good, finding my spot at the front, settling into my pace, but after 400m something felt wrong. My legs began to feel heavier and heavier. This is usually the point I start ramping up, finding a kick at the last 200m mark but this day I had nothing! No kick, no speed, absolutely no sprint to give in the last 100m. I kept searching inside myself for that little extra but I was completely empty: the other athletes were passing me and I literally felt like I was going backwards. I kid you not when I say I felt like I could have walked the last 100m faster. I finished the race and I felt so sick and so awful, I knew something was wrong: this was not me, I could barely breathe. You may assume that's normal at the end of a race, well not for me! I used to walk off the track huffing and puffing, yes, but not like I couldn't breathe and never feeling like I was about to throw up.

I walked off the track and found a place out of the way where I could throw up, only I never did. I just kept retching and desperately wanting to cry but there were people everywhere, I needed to keep it in and shut it down.

It was a league event and I was asked to run the 400m. I said I couldn't, I didn't feel right, but they kept asking and eventually I gave in. It was another shit race, with the same feeling and the same effect as the 800m.

Just so you can understand how off I was, here are some statistics: my PB for 800m is 2:11.91 (two minutes, eleven seconds and ninety-one hundredths of a second), but that day I ran 2:21.85, and my 400m PB is 58:9 (fifty-eighty seconds and nine tenths of a second), and that day I ran it in 64:74. The whole season had gone this way. A few weeks before this race, my 800m time was 2:26. I hadn't run that slowly since I started doing 800m races in 2004.

This was the summer I met Lee. A few days after this race I was in the back of Lee's car with my friend as we were super cool spinning around town. This friend had been with me throughout much of my running and personal life. I looked at her, and out of the blue – and in such a calm voice – I said something along the lines of 'I can't race any more, I'm done.' She looked at me in shock, not quite knowing what to say. And just like that, I never raced again. I can't remember ever consciously thinking this before that very moment, yet it was so true when I said it. I also recall Lee saying something that infuriated me, he was so dismissive and seemed to think I wanted to spend my summer spinning around town and hanging out with my friends, instead of training and racing. We weren't together at this point, I hardly knew him, he was just my friend's friend and that moment made me dislike him even more! He didn't know me as an athlete and the way he thought it was no big deal just irritated the shit out of me.

I continued to spiral. My dad had left at this point and now I was battling something else, something I couldn't see or understand. I ended up spending that summer getting drunk most weekends, I even tried smoking as a way to have control over something, but it only lasted about two weeks because I really hated the taste, especially the morning after. It really did seem completely pointless. I even smoked weed one night in an attempt to stop my pain. I was at a point of *What's the fucking point? I can't run any more, does it really matter if I drink, smoke or do drugs?*

Luckily, when I do stupid things like this, I (thankfully) have a moment of realisation at some point before I get in too deep. The way I describe it is like someone is looking after me and I feel this silence not just in my mind but in my body too: it's completely different to my normal inner dialogue, which can be so chaotic, obsessed with everything going wrong. Back then my inner thoughts were constantly angry; all I wanted to do was scream at the world. But this, this silence was like the calm within the storm, it was always so clear, so calming and always felt so true. That is the part that has always come to save me.

So much changed in those few weeks. After a bit of a rocky start, thinking this guy called Lee was an absolute twat and potentially a liar, I eventually came around and agreed to go out with him. When he first asked me out my thoughts were, *I have no idea what is going on with me, my house is up for sale so I probably won't be sticking around here.* The ultimate barrier was I have always seen boyfriends as drama. Obviously seeing it with my parents but also my friends, and I just didn't want to deal with someone else's feelings on top of my own. And I made that VERY clear to him. He didn't seem to mind one bit and told me it was love at first sight. I kind of wish I could say the same now because how cute would that story be, instead, I have the memory of thinking he was a complete arse.

After *finally* agreeing to give the relationship a go I stayed at his house for 2 nights. My pain was now getting worse, and the stabbing pains in my head were now in my stomach too. Intense, severe shooting pains. He stayed up with me most of the night making sure I was OK. For me, this was a standard night. However, it was the first time I felt someone genuinely cared and was there for me. It was a very weird feeling. Although I still couldn't express myself and I made everything into a joke. Every time I said something with a bit of sincerity I would quickly glaze over it with a witty remark, which if you haven't noticed by now is because I'm fucking hilarious, but it's also my safety mechanism. Humour covered the true pain and fear behind what I was really feeling.

After three days of being together, he stayed at my house as my mum was away visiting her dad and I wasn't a fan of staying in our house on my own, and, well, Lee just never left. Even when I went to university he lived with my mum. Three weeks into our relationship he told me he wanted to marry me and I nearly fell off my chair. He said it again at three months and again at six months: by this point I knew I wanted to marry him too, but I was so worried about what other people would think and that they would see it as something that wouldn't last because we were so young.

When we were on our first holiday together, I said 'we should wait until we'd been together for at least one year', but once he knew I would say yes he wouldn't stop talking about it. He asked if I would pick my own ring as he thought he'd pick the wrong one and I actually loved that he asked because I was finally being asked what I wanted. I picked the ring (my mum paid for it and Lee made payments to my mum until he paid it off). Ten months after we first got together, he took me to the beach to get me out of the house. It was the same beach where we'd always go for fish and chips. That's where he proposed. OK, so it wasn't actually on the beach; it was in the Land Rover, but I wouldn't change one second of it because it was just so Lee. I still remember the look on his face, and it makes my heart so full every time I think of that moment. It was also Lee who encouraged me to try and rebuild my relationship with my dad, which I did, slowly over time.

A lot happened over the next few years, which I want to summarise for you now because they were huge, life-changing events, but the main focus of this book is me and my chronic illness, not *This Is Your Life*, the Katie Parkes edition. We got engaged when I was eighteen and I gave birth to our first child at age twenty. We had a daughter, Isabelle. The pregnancy started off OK but by the end I was in one of the worst flare-ups I'd ever had. I could barely move due to the fatigue. I ended up having a C-section because I could only just function with daily life. I then ended up with postnatal depression and felt completely and utterly detached from this beautiful baby girl. There was just so much fear in me: I had to not only keep myself fed and alive, I also had a tiny human who depended on me. I just didn't know how or if I could do it.

Lee and I got married later that year. We went to Saint Lucia, just the two of us and it was absolutely beautiful. We aren't ones for big, fancy weddings and I dreaded people looking at me, so just the two of us was perfect. We had a party when we came home for friends and family, so I got to wear my wedding dress twice.

I then had a second baby at twenty-two, a son this time, called Matthew. That pregnancy went better as I was doing better in myself, but then I faced the battle of having two little ones under the age of two. It didn't help that Lee was struggling at the time with the responsibility of being a dad and husband: he seemed to think he could go off whenever he fancied, even though I'd be home all day with the kids. It was like he wanted to be married and a parent but at the same time have no responsibilities at all. We really struggled in our marriage at this point.

I had to find something to do for myself, I was going stir crazy being a stay-at-home parent who could scarcely function some days and then on the good days had fuck all to do. So I started my own handmade sterling silver jewellery business at twenty-three. I loved it. I loved creating things from nothing, I loved learning something new, I loved challenging myself. I did that for quite a few years, until I got so poorly with tremors and spasms that I had to stop, everything just became too much, which you will read about further on in the book.

CHAPTER 4

It's Not Just My Story

It's yours

This book is not a 'woe is me' story, I can see the positives and negatives of my story. Yes, it was shit to live through but I also believe everything happens for a reason and that I would not be who I am today if I hadn't experienced all that I have. How boring would it have been if life had just been easy! Yawn, right?! Challenges and hardship make us stronger when we know how to turn it into a superpower rather than be consumed by it.

I love to learn and grow from past experiences. To understand how things from our past shape us, and affect our decisions to make progress moving forward. I think it is a gift to be able to learn and pass that knowledge down to the next generation, who can then continue to learn and grow themselves and pass on their learnings. That to me is the definition of *knowledge is power!*

I want you to understand that I didn't know any of what I'll be sharing with you until about eight years after my diagnosis. Until that point, I lived in a perpetual state of survival, living each day like it was Groundhog Day. I had no idea that there was a possibility of something more for me out there. I didn't even have the thought of being able to get better, to look for something that could help me because I was always told it wasn't possible, so why would I look if everyone told me there's nothing that can help, that I just had to adjust my life around my symptoms.

So I just kept battling each day to get up out of bed, to show up for my family. I have to say having kids most definitely saved me many times over. I think I would have withered away if I didn't have them. They gave me a purpose, a reason to get out of bed in the morning. They were my spark, my fight.

I don't want you to be like me, just surviving, being a living ghost in people's lives, hiding your pain, feeling like a burden and ashamed of who you've become. No, no more! I want you to challenge the beliefs of others and yourself, to ask questions, to seek your own answers and form your own, new beliefs rather than just taking what others say as fact, especially if they've not lived what you have. Find your own discoveries, do research, ask questions. There is still so much more out there that I don't know yet. Maybe you'll find something I've not come across yet. You won't know unless you try.

I share my story because I know this is not just my story, it is also yours. It might not be the same cause or the same effect that you experience, but when you break it all down to the core, to the root causes, you begin to see that we are, in fact, all the same. Living a life based on the coping mechanisms that we developed as children to survive this funny little thing called life!

You are not alone!

I will break down what you need to know about yourself and your illness by sharing my own realisations, thoughts and healing processes. Uncovering the things I went through so you can really see how you are an intricate being who has simply not been taught the power of the mind and body and that you do in fact hold the key to your own wellbeing! I want you to be open to the fact that what you currently believe and think about yourself is not actually the truth of you. It is based on many illusions and survival strategies. You can think of them as false layers of truth, or as I like to call them: *lies!*

You didn't know that you absorbed these false truths and took them on as the truth. This version of you was created as a way to survive the situation at the time with the resources that you had at the time. As children we do not have many resources, other than those modelled to us by those around us as we grow up. And I'm sure you're aware that your caregivers were not perfect, no one is. I want to shine a light on the illusions you've been carrying with you every day.

I began learning that we are basically a shitload of layers (yes, that's right, we are just like Shrek: we, too, are just like onions). Those layers developed from the ego mind, absorbing what was around you from the day you were born, even before you were born as you absorbed the theme of consciousness (a filter or lens in which you see the world through) your mother was in as she carried you to term. I'll explain more about the themes of consciousness towards the end of the book chapter 31.

Simply put, if your mum is in a bad relationship, maybe she feels unlovable and tells herself things like, *I'm not good enough, I'm ugly, I hate myself, I hate my life,* then you absorb those thoughts into your being. How? Because everything is vibration, even thoughts. I go deeper into vibrations and the power of words later in chapter 20.

You may understand this better by recalling times when you have been sitting with someone and say exactly what they were thinking or about to say. Or you ring someone and they say 'I was just about to ring you!' Everything is connected. Our human, ego minds just find it hard to comprehend that this could be true because it is not something we can physically see. I'll explain more about the ego mind in just a moment.

When you are a foetus, you obviously don't know that the vibrations you are absorbing are not yours, it just feels like it's yours because it is what surrounds you through your development. It is familiar, it is what you believe to be true on an energetic and unconscious level. That is why there may be parts of you that feel like you've always felt this way, never really understanding where it came from … because it was never yours in the first place. This is how we can end up repeating the same patterns and cycles as our parents. You then continue to absorb more false truths as you grow up. These layers are a result of not making decisions for yourself about who you are or who you want to be; they come from someone else. Consequently, you take on someone else's pain, traumas and conditioning.

Learning this allowed me to finally start seeing and understanding the truth. That what I believed about myself was not actually who I was at all: it was something I'd been told over and over again or I'd absorbed through surrounding vibrations until this belief system became my own. This is why I wish we were taught all this growing up, this knowledge helps you to break through the blocks that may be holding you back from your own healing. This is why I'm sharing this now, because even though you may not fully understand what I'm saying just yet, your mind is taking it in at an unconscious level. These words will already be working their way through some pre-existing programming, opening your mind, or you may feel it challenging you. You may even feel a resistance to some of what I share. That is very normal because it is challenging your current belief system and that is what you need to begin to move forward and start to heal.

Traumas, programming and beliefs are not always projected towards you by words alone, but by body language, a facial expression, the way someone walks towards you, or isolates you. Sometimes words are not even used at all. It all hurts the same. They all provoke the ego mind into protecting you. How does it do that? By creating a coping mechanism or strategy that will keep you safe and protected, such as keeping your mouth shut and/or not expressing your opinions.

Another way trauma can be created is by the use of words that don't seem hurtful, malicious or cruel, yet the tone in which they are spoken tells you all you need to know. We are energetic beings, there is so much that we pick up and sense every minute of every day. Think of a time when you've walked into a room and you just know that there has been an argument, because you feel it, you sense it in the air. The same when you walk into a room and instantly feel lifted by someone as they greet you, because again you sense the energy that person provides; it affects your energy. It is all vibrations and intentions. We are surrounded by so much unseen energy and we've no idea we are absorbing all this shit as we go through our days, affecting how you feel – hell it even affects your cells and *so* much more.

THE EGO MIND

Before we move on, I think it's important to understand the ego. I always associated the ego with someone being big-headed and loving attention from others. There is so much more to it than that. There are books dedicated to the working of the ego mind but I'd like to introduce it with the simplest explanation I can to help you as you continue to read the book.

The ego mind is the part of your consciousness that is concerned with your self-image and identity, and creates a sense of individuality or persona. It is the voice in your head that tells you who you are and how you relate and react to the world around you, the way in which you see the world. It is the conditioned self, or you may hear it referred to as the false self, as it is not who you truly are at your core. It feeds off fear and lives through the lens of a win, lose mentality.

It's the part of you that thinks, 'I am this' or 'I want that' and is always seeking to protect and enhance your sense of self, known as your identity. The ego mind is formed from attaching to our past experiences and beliefs. It can often be driven by fear and a desire to protect yourself. It can lead you to identify with certain labels, such as your job title or social status, and can create attachments to things like material possessions or relationships.

While the ego mind can be helpful in certain circumstances, such as keeping you safe in dangerous situations, it can sometimes cause you to become overly attached to your own beliefs and desires, preventing you from seeing things objectively or from other people's perspectives.

Because it can only work from past experiences, it essentially bases everything on your memory, the database you hold inside. It is why you find yourself dwelling on things, and thoughts play on repeat, flooding your mind, especially when you try to fall asleep: this is your ego mind trying to figure things out. Analysing, preparing, wondering how to be and do better next time. Why? Because the ego is all about surviving, about being better, doing better than everyone else, being superior.

Basing all its knowledge on past experiences means the ego mind perceives the future as something scary, an unknown, because there's no database to pull from. Consequently, it can create fear or anxiety of the future as a way to keep you safe, to keep you in what you know, even if you're in pain, have no energy and can barely talk. It is protecting you.

This protective instinct, however, can limit you and cause you to live in a place of suffering. By becoming more aware of our ego and its patterns, you can work to transcend it and connect with a deeper sense of self, leading you to develop greater self-awareness, empathy for others and begin to move out of suffering.

EXERCISE – THE TREE OF YOU

Let's get to work straight away on that sense of self-awareness and truth, by reminding yourself who you are under the layers.

This is a space for you to write down all the things that bring you joy, including from when you were younger. The things you may have enjoyed at one time until maybe someone told you that you weren't good enough, or your friends thought it was childish.

This is about YOU! If you want to include your family or friends then write them as one group, don't fill each branch with an individual. For example, you might have one branch which says 'family' and another that says 'dancing' or 'walking'.

Each branch is a part of what makes you, you. You are not defined as one thing. You are made up of many moving parts. It's time to honour all parts of yourself. When you need reminding of who you are, come back to this page. Pick something from one of your branches and bring some joy into your day once more.

CHAPTER 5

Uncover Not Recover

Let me explain what this means before you start ganging up on me. You may have picked up this book because you saw I have 'recovered' from an illness that we are constantly told you cannot recover from. Maybe you have seen that there was a time I could barely do anything for myself and now I do it all and more and you want that for yourself too. Great! I am so here for that and it's why I wrote this book. However, the truth is, my journey has not been a journey of recovering, it has been a journey of *uncovering* and that, my friend, is not an easy journey to take but it is one that is worth every bit of discomfort along the way.

Of course, it would be amazing if I said 'You just need to do this or take that and bam! You're cured!' I would have killed for something as simple as that back in the day.

How many times have you said *I just want to recover, to be the person I used to be?* I used to say this all the time, I was grieving the person I once was, which left me resentful and carrying so much pain for the person who was snatched away from me. It took me *years* before I finally gave up trying to run again. I even remember the day I finally told myself to stop trying altogether and that it was time to accept it will never be a part of my life.

It was a few months after Matthew was born, which was in 2012, so I'd already spent about four years battling with myself, hoping, not wanting to let go of that part of myself. The identity I knew so well, the part of myself I escaped into. I put on my running clothes, I felt hopeful and so good as I stepped out the front door on a somewhat sunny day. I began running along the road and turned off onto the country lane. The wind against my skin, the bounce in every step, a smile on my face with every pound of the pavement. It felt so freeing, so uplifting, it was like I could breathe for the first time in a long time. I didn't go far and it was all flat, which is very rare around our area.

I came home and felt good. Until a few hours later when the fatigue started to creep in. Over the course of the next month I was back to barely being able to move my body. Lifting my head became so unbelievably challenging, let alone moving around the house. Then came the sharp pains, the frustration, the anger as I tried to look after two small humans. All I wanted to do was curl up and disappear. I was so angry with myself for going for that run; if I hadn't, I wouldn't be suffering that badly. I would have just had my normal fatigue, my normal pains, I'd be able to function better, to think clearly. That's when I decided I was done trying.

After that, I used to pray, pray that it would just all go away, that I could just be a normal person again. I wouldn't be greedy, I didn't have to run again; I wanted to exist without feeling like every breath, every movement was destroying me slowly from the inside out, it was utterly crippling. Then there were days I'd hear so-and-so had said *She's just lazy, it's all an act, she's not that bad, she just doesn't want to work and just want everything handed to her.* Sound familiar? Those words cut deep but I wouldn't let myself show the world how much it hurt. I would laugh and say *Well they can say what they want, I know the truth.* But the truth was I would start to let those words swirl around my mind and I'd start to question if they were true.

I knew deep down they weren't true at all. I knew those comments came from people who saw me on my good days because those were the *only* days I'd let myself leave the house. Good days were days I felt I had enough energy to slap a smile on my face and put on my armour of humour. The smile and humour protected me in those moments. I still felt a tug deep within me that wanted to crumble and shout for help, for anyone to just take away this pain inside me but that would be an inconvenience to others so I must smile, laugh and joke so everyone else can feel comfortable.

I do remember those comments becoming quieter when I started to share my story, to share my truth about what I was really dealing with on the days I didn't leave the house, what actually lurked behind closed doors. I shared it on social media, though I didn't share it all. I shared the physical impact but not the deeper, darker layers, the parts of myself I hid from everyone else (myself included) … until now.

I finally realised it was the idea of the old me I missed; I held that version of myself on a pedestal. Looking all shiny and new and full of confidence, who didn't care when her friends made fun of her for wanting to run. I craved the able-bodied part of myself, the energy she possessed and I also missed the praise and admiration I got from being a successful athlete, that ego boost that made me feel worthy. The truth is that the idealisation of who I used to be was a dream, a dream where I thought I could go back and undo time.

If I recovered back to that version of myself, I would quickly learn that that young girl was not full of energy, confident or even felt worthy at all because when you put someone on a pedestal, even yourself, then you begin to set unobtainable expectations and your mind amplifies the idea of what could have been and forgets the parts that weren't so good.

If I had made it back to that version without addressing any of the emotional wounds that she carried, then what led to the illness in the first place would still have been there, lingering, bubbling away under the surface. Later in life it would have just appeared again because emotions live in the mind and body when they're not fully processed, so they would still have come out eventually – maybe in a different way but something would have happened.

Ultimately, I was still that naïve little girl who held her parents on a pedestal, seeing herself smaller than everyone else, too afraid to speak her mind and stand up for what she wanted. Too afraid to upset anyone, always weighing the pros and cons, always trying to see every side of a story in case she backed the wrong person, which was inevitable because that's just being human.

However, to me, being wrong meant I was a failure, I wasn't good enough, I wasn't worthy. I was so scared of speaking and any time I did try I would end up crying because there was so much bubbling beneath the surface. And that was before I was even ill. I just couldn't find my words … no, I didn't know the words. I was never taught them, which led to frustration, which led to tears. I'd tried so damn hard to keep everything together as I spoke my truth but my truth was foreign, so unknown that my body would react, like I was being attacked. Shaking, ready to run, but paralysed!

I call recovering 're-covering' because, to me, recovering is just putting a plaster on something, hiding the real issues that lie underneath it all. Think of it like every time you hold your tongue, put on a smile to hide your pain, or make someone laugh as a way to deflect, you're actually just placing a blanket over yourself, a layer to hide the truth behind the smile and jokes. Think about how heavy that becomes, carrying all those blankets around with you every day. Tiring, right? Exhausting, overwhelming, making you want to hide in your own physical blanket and not get out of bed. That is the reality of re-covering: you hide, you avoid, you become scared of your own truth, scared of what may be hiding under all those layers.

Uncovering, on the other hand, is all about peeling back those false truths, those blankets. It's asking the hard questions, facing truths that we have hidden from ourselves. It is the part of ourselves that lives in the shadows, that tells us *It's too much to face, there's too much to unpack.* It is the discomfort you feel in the silence or when faced with an emotion that feels too big. However, it does lead you to the root causes and when you bring awareness to why or how your mind decided that this symptom or illness would protect you in some way or another – because it does – then you can work on creating new neural pathways to change the outcome. Your mind is malleable like that: the current way you function and work is not set in stone. It's referred to as 'remapping' or 'rewiring' the brain. I will be sharing my own discoveries to expand on this later on in the book.

To really simplify this, you can look at it like this: re-covering is cutting a plant at the stem, thinking you're cutting off the dead bit, but you leave behind the core memory it stores on how to regrow, whereas uncovering is like pulling the roots out so it has no memory of how to regrow.

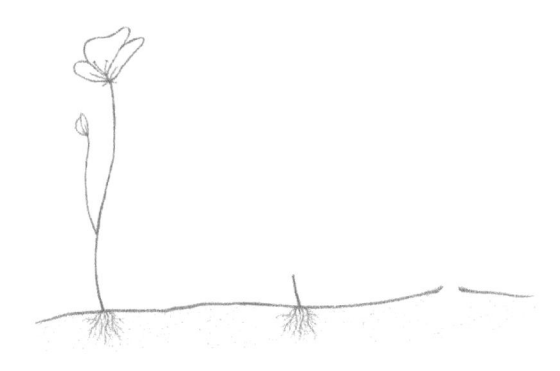

The roots hold on to the core memory. By holding on to these roots, you can't change your actions or behaviour because the messages being sent throughout the body and mind haven't changed. It's why I talk about finding the root cause because that is what you want to get to, so you can pull up those roots and plant something new.

CHAPTER 6

How I Saved Myself

How did I save myself? Through a whole load of trial and error as well as being willing and open-minded to giving anything a go. You get to that point of being sick and tired of being sick and tired, so you will literally try anything if it means it might help.

I didn't set out to do any of what I've done, I just took it one step at a time. In fact, if you told the old me that I would have my whole life back and have a whole different outlook and belief about myself and the world, I wouldn't have believed you in the slightest. Honestly, I probably would have given you a disgusting look as I rolled my eyes while telling you to *fuck off* in my head.

See, I was you. I was so convinced that this illness was it for me. Right when I was in the depths of this awful illness (2014), I was told by a psychic medium that in ten years I wouldn't have any sign of having an illness. I laughed and thought, *You're so full of shit!* A month later I had the worst flare-up ever. *Well I call bullshit on that reading!* was my instant response. I actually spiralled more because even though I didn't consciously believe her, something deep inside had been sparked, only to be drowned out. Yet here we are, ten years later, and she was fucking right! You would never know now that for fourteen years I'd been unable to care for myself.

What actually happened here is that being told I could be well again triggered my ego mind and emotional body, because it didn't align with my belief system: it wasn't true in the past so it can't be true of the future. Now the ego has to protect me from this 'threat'. How does it do that? By proving the belief right, so here comes the flare-up. Obviously, I had no idea this was happening because it is all going on deeper in the mind, on an unconscious level, just running those past programs.

The information I've shared with you so far about the truth behind the ego, the mind and the body, and how the cause and effect of childhood carries through to adulthood is what I wish was taught throughout childhood. I think I would have done a few things differently if I'd known and maybe even saved a hell of a lot of time and money along the way.

However, I am a massive believer in everything happens for a reason and everything reveals itself when you are ready. There's a saying that one man's medicine is another man's poison. Which was explained to me in this way … if I gave you advice right now from the place I am currently in, but you're at the beginning of your journey, maybe you're in the place I was on that sofa, then that same advice could be a trigger for you. It could anger you and make you want to punch me in the face. And I get it because I have had that advice at the wrong times, times I wasn't ready to hear it. And this book could do that to you as you read new things that set off your ego mind's need to protect you, just like mine did after seeing the psychic medium. And that is OK, you need to be challenged, you need to get uncomfortable. You cannot grow while living in the comfort of what you currently know, living with the same unhelpful habits, running on automatic, outdated programs from your unconscious that are just so familiar that you think you don't know how to live without them.

For now, take what resonates and leave everything else behind. As you continue on your journey you may find yourself rereading this book and seeing it from a whole different perspective, a new lens, through a different filter of life. You're constantly developing and growing and you can change your beliefs and opinions at any time. It all comes down to choice.

This journey of trying all these different things led me down a path that ultimately allowed me to save myself and YOU can save yourself too! I truly believe that with all my heart.

I believe if we were just taught the truth about the mind, body and spirit then millions of people would not be suffering as they are now. And I know it can be hard to really and truly believe that there is a world where you can be symptom-free after living years or even decades as you have been. If you're not ready to believe you can have your health back fully then why not grant yourself permission for a slightly healthier life, a better quality than you have right now. It's exactly how I started. Remember, I didn't set off on a quest to heal, to have my life back. I just wanted a better quality of life.

Maybe this book is your starting point, or maybe it's your next step, maybe it peels back a layer or two that you've been drowning in, just like I was. I share my experiences because I know deep down that this is what I'm supposed to do. It's why I started sharing what I was going through behind closed doors. Granted, I can now see I was still hiding so much of my own truth – not on purpose, not consciously, I just wasn't able to admit to myself that I was hurting so much, that I was in a deep dark hole filled with hatred, anger and the silent cries of *Why the fuck is this happening to me?* I buried that shit deep; I plastered on a smile and I made jokes about my tremors and crawling along the floor. I did this for so many reasons: one was to protect myself from myself, if I'd felt all that was really going on I wouldn't be here right now, it was just too much to handle. Another reason was to protect my family: I already felt like a massive burden and if they knew the true internal battle going on then they wouldn't leave me in the house on my own or they'd constantly worry all of the time about me. They already worried enough and did enough for me, so I couldn't bring myself to tell them.

CHAPTER 7

The Very Beginning

Previously, I shared with you my personal experience of how trauma manifested within my physical being and some of the mental battles I fought. I am about to share my account from my diagnosis to being symptom-free, sharing the highs and the lows, the powerful realisations and lessons I learnt along the way, as well the tools and techniques that you, too, can use in your everyday life.

I was in university when I was eventually diagnosed with M.E./CFS in 2008 by our local doctor (the one I mentioned in chapter 3, Dr Roberts). All blood tests had come back 'normal', including an in depth private blood test I had done. I'd never heard of M.E./CFS but one of my housemates was already convinced I had it, as she knew someone who had it and suffered just like I did, but I didn't want to accept it because it was something unknown, something I'd never heard of. Plus, this person had had it for years which was even scarier. Years … I couldn't have this for years!

When I was first diagnosed, Mum and I researched everything we could about M.E., because – like most who are diagnosed with a chronic illness – once diagnosed you are left to your own devices to live with it. There is no support or advice on how to even begin to come to terms with the diagnosis, let alone how to heal from it (or at least there wasn't back in 2008).

When we found the M.E. Association website we thought we'd found something that would help us, help me. We expected to find answers, information, some advice on how to manage the illness. However, it was not what I was hoping for. Everything I read was telling me this is it, there is no cure, it's something you have to adjust your life around. Everywhere I looked was telling me the same things. Feeding my mind with a story that I would continue to tell myself over and over again for years. When medical professionals and others who suffer with the same illness all tell you the same thing there isn't much space left for hope, for something different, because surely if there was a way to get better they would have found it by now.

My eighteen-year-old self was so confused, *What do you mean this is it? What is graded exercise therapy? But I'll still be able to run, right? What am I supposed to do now?* Everything I knew about myself was falling apart and crashing down around me. I felt so deflated and alone.

One of the main reasons for going to university was literally so I could be closer to my coach for training sessions, to have access to proper training facilities nearby, unlike where I lived which was (as my dear friend said) in the arse-end of nowhere. Being an athlete was my whole world, who would I be without it? What would I do? I have never been that kid who knows exactly what they want to be when they are older. I always came up blank. I saw my future in sport, maybe as a physio, a coach or something I could do alongside training. But if I couldn't run, if I was wiped out from just walking home from campus then what would be left of me?

When I was first diagnosed, I honestly didn't believe it was going to affect my life. I just figured it was like a virus. My body was being attacked and I just needed to rest up and I'd get over it. Simple.

Oh, how wrong I was. I have always lived on the more optimistic side of life but this may have been closer to a delusional side.

The symptoms were already affecting me way more than I liked to admit. Each week at university, I'd get to Wednesday, occasionally Thursdays, and then the stabbing pains and dull ache would grow and grow, which led to extreme fatigue, brain fog and many, many tears. By the Friday I would ring my mum or Lee in such a state, crying my eyes out because I was in so much pain and I felt so alone, and Lee would drive two hours in the middle of the night to come get me. I'd then return to university on the Sunday evening, determined to try again, but each week the cycle was the same.

I kept trying to get back to running as well because, like I said, the whole point of me going to university was so I could be closer to my coach for training while studying sports biomedicine and nutrition. I loved the science behind things and obviously sport was my thing, but I just kept failing and making my symptoms worse.

After six months, I ended up dropping out of university. Initially, deciding to leave felt like a huge relief. But eventually it left me feeling hollow and like I was a failure. Powerful moment right here, right now in fact as I write, which I'm going to share as it's happening.

As I was writing, recalling how I felt at that time I noticed a tension in my body as I wrote that I felt 'hollow' and a 'failure'. These are feelings I've never paired with leaving university because it did feel like a huge relief.

When I sat with that realisation for a second, I had an 'aha!' moment as to why no matter how many courses and trainings I do, I feel like I need to learn more, do more. So now I'm curious and want to pick this apart. This is when I do self-enquiry, or inner work as some call it. I find myself asking the following questions:

1. What does another course get me?

   It gives me knowledge.

2. How does that knowledge benefit me?

   Knowledge means I know what I'm talking about, it means I have worth, that I can back up what I say.

3. What's the need in being able to back up what I say?

   I need to feel good enough, to be seen on the same level as someone who has a 'proper' education, a degree.

4. Why do I need to be seen on the same level as someone with a degree?

   Because I don't have one and people look up to those with an education and a degree. It would give me value, respect.

And there it is. The limiting belief that has kept me searching for more and more. When in reality the knowledge I've accumulated over the years – through many courses like NLP, sound healing, reiki, yoga – paired with my own experiences is more than enough. Of course, there is always more to learn and discover, whether that is through challenges life gives us, through courses or just being ready to receive new information, but I finally realised I don't need a degree to be enough. I am enough!

How was this limiting belief created in the first place? It comes from societal conditioning. We grow up in an educational system that praises the outcomes of tests over life skills and real-life experiences. We're taught that you go from one educational institute to another and another until you have the 'proper' education needed to be able to get a 'proper' job. We're taught that if we don't have the right education then we are not good enough and are only able to dream of small, adequate jobs that suit our educational level. Well, I call bullshit!

I'm not saying all education is crap and no one should do it. Absolutely do it if it is what *you* want. If you know what you want to do with your life then go after it with all you have. Just don't do it because you feel you *should* or because that's what everyone else is doing.

After I left university, I moved back home to my mum's house, where Lee and I lived in the summer house in the garden. It used to be my training space but obviously that wasn't needed any more and it honestly hurt to look at it, set up for something I could no longer do.

So we changed it into a cute little home. It had two rooms where we could have a bedroom in one space and a kitchen/front room in the other space. We even had a pull-out sofa so friends could crash there if needed. I always felt so at home there; it was so peaceful and I went about my days trying not to overdo things and save as much of my energy as I could. And it was working. After a month or two I was starting to feel better and I found hope beginning to brew; I was on the mend.

While everyone was working during the day, I found a manageable routine that worked for me. Doing a few things but nothing too crazy as it was a very delicate balance with the amount of energy that was available to me.

Once I'd established this routine and felt like I could actively try to get better, I bought what seemed like the entire range of supplements from Holland & Barrett. This was part of my effort to try everything I could think of, feeding my body whatever it might be lacking so it could start working properly again. I was able to go for walks and occasionally even little jogs when my body felt good. I had a workout DVD that I loved by Mel B ... I believed her every time she told me I was doing amazing and no matter how many times I'd done it, she still made me laugh even though I knew exactly what she was going to say. I felt so much hope in that space, in those moments; I truly believed I was going to get my life back, which meant running and competing. That was my only focus.

I thought that was it: the start of my recovery. Oh, how life had a different plan. Over time my world would get smaller and smaller, to the point where I'd rarely see anyone. Friends would go on to live their lives, with contact between us becoming less and less until eventually all I would have was Lee and Mum. No wonder I became such a co-dependent, anxious mess who felt numb and alone all the time.

CHAPTER 8

The Specialist

What a waste of time

While I was still in university, my mum had been researching everything she could to help me. Let's not forget it wasn't like it is today where you can just google everything and find page after page of information. There wasn't much around back then, especially on M.E./CFS: hardly anyone had heard of it, including many doctors.

Somehow my mum managed to find a specialist in M.E./CFS. Even better, they were based in Wales! What a stroke of luck! *And* he was just above Cardiff, right near my university. Bloody perfect!

My mum scraped together the £150 needed for the consultation. She only recently told me what she meant by 'scraped' it together. You know when you were a kid and you'd check the sofas for loose change so you could claim it for yourself? It was essentially that on a household scale: checking all the money jars, old purses and bags. Although my brother wasn't living at home at this point, he helped out by giving Mum his money pot. I had no idea he'd contributed towards this fee until I started writing this book. My mum even sold some of her gold jewellery.

The appointment was booked and we were actually excited: I was going to see someone who specialised in what I had, someone who could give me answers and directions in how I could overcome this.

The actual day is mostly a blur. I remember the stress of trying to find the correct junction to exit the motorway and then the next thing

I remember is sitting in a room that felt dark. There was wood furnishing (stained dark), a wall of books and then those chairs that you see in films, the ones where there's usually an old guy with a pipe sitting in them, next to a fireplace. Finally, there was this big wooden desk with a gentleman sitting behind it.

Now I know the appointment went on for longer than the five minutes I remember, however, I remember this particular bit because it was like a punch to the stomach. This specialist had been talking about the cyclists he had been helping (so I was thinking, *Yes! He helps other athletes like me*) only for him to turn around and say I should get this book and that book, showing us these heavy university-style books to understand the mindset and the mechanisms of the body. It was like someone just sucked out all the hope I had, with me left thinking, *How can reading five big ass books heal me? This is fucking bullshit. That won't help me run again or get rid of these stabbing pains or give me more energy. What am I supposed to do with fucking books?* I could only just about make a noodle packet for lunch after reading the packet three times. Brain fog had become so bad that retaining any information felt like an impossible mission. I don't think even Tom Cruise would have been able to complete that mission: he'd barely remember reading the top-secret file.

The irony of it all is he wasn't wrong in what he said about learning more about mindset. He just had a terrible approach in how he communicated the information. It was like he had no understanding of what M.E./CFS even was, if he thought I had the energy and mental capacity to read such massive books with all that overwhelming information. That's the funny thing about all this: I've learnt that no one fully understands unless they themselves have been through it, which can then lead to you feeling completely alone.

It wasn't long after this appointment I dropped out of university, which I described in the previous chapter. *Everything* was just too hard. Socialising with the girls I was living with was exhausting, let alone cooking for myself. I felt like I was just a body walking around, like I was no longer present, in an almost constant state of dissociation.

Now it seemed my only option was to adjust my life to accommodate my symptoms.

I rarely saw any doctors again after this, especially after Dr Roberts passed away – the only one who really knew me and also the only doctor in the surgery who believed in M.E./CFS. Whenever I saw any other doctor it was an absolute battle to even get them to believe in my diagnosis. They just saw me as a young person who was trying to get out of working and wanting everything handed to them.

I even had one doctor who had never heard of M.E./CFS, so he had to google it and then look it up in a book. He was nice though, at least he tried and was honest that because he didn't know anything about this condition, there was nothing he could do other than give me painkillers.

Another doctor told me point blank he did not believe in this condition, so I replied with 'That's absolutely fine, I am open to hearing an alternative to what this might be.' I actually left that appointment with a tiny bit of hope – which is odd I know, seeing as he didn't even believe I had M.E./CFS, but I couldn't help but think how great it would be if it was something else that could be fixed.

He proceeded with a few tests and I returned to my next appointment wondering what I was going to be diagnosed with after all these years. Only to be met with 'Well, it seems you do have M.E./CFS!' *Are you fucking kidding me?!* Another punch in the gut and yet again no help or support. Just sent on my merry way to attempt to live with an illness that seemed to be getting worse with every year that passed and not one doctor who gave a shit about what it was doing to me mentally, let alone the physical pain, brain fog and fatigue.

So back I went to just surviving best I could.

CHAPTER 9

Neurologist

There are no words

My body still tenses and my eyes still roll at the thought of my experience with the neurologist. I was mentally punching her right in the face and screaming, *you fucking arsehole, you're supposed to help me figure this shit out, why won't you help me, what did I do to deserve this, being made to feel like I'm making all this shit up, why would I do that, what would I gain ... AARGH!*

Why did I see a neurologist? Well, my spectacular body decided I was getting too comfortable with the symptoms I already had and decided to gift me yet another symptom: muscle spasms and tremors, because well, why the hell not. It wasn't like I was doing anything else! I swear the universe was laughing at me and thought it would be fun to watch and see what would happen.

It was about 2014 when they first started, six years after my diagnosis, and I was living with my mum (... because when am I not). At first, I thought they were funny, mostly because it started with a numb muscle in my leg. It was weird and occasionally my leg would give out, only for a split second, every few steps. We called it 'gangster styling' because I looked like I had a right attitude coming towards you with my 'swag'.

After about a month or so it started to progress into this weird shaking and I looked like I was trying to twerk while walking, which again made me laugh and I would think, *If I just put on some headphones it would look like I'm bopping away to music; no one needs to know I'm not doing it on purpose.* However, it was soon happening every time I walked and it became exhausting for my body. My legs became heavier and heavier, my breathing was affected, so walking became harder and harder with every day that passed.

I'd been living with this new symptom for a few months and getting around Mum's house was getting more difficult, especially the stairs. I was home alone most days while everyone was out working and the kids were in school. We decided to look for a place that was more suitable for my rollercoaster of a body. I needed to have a bathroom downstairs so I didn't have to fight my way to the toilet each day. At this point I was still somehow walking around, regardless of the shaking. I think it was mostly because I always thought, *They'll go away in a minute; they won't last too long.* My god I was still in denial even when presented with the facts. Looking back, I laugh at how much I believed it at the time, knowing the years and the battles this would lead me to face. But nope, I just had to believe it would just all go away. You've got to love a bit of denial to get you through life, right?

God forbid if someone asked if I needed help, however. I'd reply very sharply with 'I'm fine!' because if I accepted help then it meant I wasn't OK, that I was failing and that this was really happening to me. I loved to live in a world of self-denial. No wonder I loved films that had fantasy worlds: I'd been living in my own version for years. It gave me a sense of safety and comfort.

We found a house with the downstairs bathroom I needed and moved in. It was also built with wheelchair accessibility, which turned out to be a godsend. The kids loved this house: their bedrooms were huge and there was plenty of space for them to play. Not long after moving into the new house my legs seemed to think, *This girl will not listen to us, she will not stop, she just keeps walking around like nothing is happening ... has she even seen what she looks like?!*

One day, I fell to the floor like a sack of potatoes. My first reaction was to laugh – it is my default setting after all. I tried to get back up but my legs wouldn't hold me, it was as if my legs were made of spaghetti – cooked of course. They were mocking me with, *Not today, bitch. Not today! [insert witch's cackle] Let's see you try and walk now.* I know now that my body was trying to communicate with me, however I didn't speak 'body', I just thought my body was being an absolute arsehole for no apparent reason.

I sat there on the cold kitchen floor thinking, *My legs will start working again in a minute.* I tried again ... and again ... and again, holding on to the kitchen island for leverage, pulling myself up with everything I had in my arms, until this wave of fear started to wash over me as I realised I was going to be stuck on the kitchen floor for the rest of the day. *How was I going to make a cup of tea and breakfast?* were my first thoughts – because priorities.

I began searching my mind for ideas of how I could make it through the day on my own. *Could I pull myself up on the kitchen chair? But then I wouldn't be able to move from the island, so no access to food or drink. Was anyone coming over today ...? Nope. Fuck. What do I do? Where's my phone?* The relief when I remembered my phone was on the worktop. Shimmying my body over was exhausting because as I tried to move my whole body started to shake: it wasn't just my legs, it was everything.

I knew I had to ring Lee but I felt guilt rising because I thought my legs would boost back up in a minute and he would have left work for no reason. And, if I'm really honest, admitting I wasn't OK would mean I'd become even more of a burden to him than I already was.

Finally, I had to admit to myself that this wasn't going away and that this may in fact be my new normal and that was terrifying. I'd already been living small, unable to take my kids to their friend's parties, barely able to see my own friends or leave the house. Accepting this meant I was useless, insignificant in the lives of those around me, just a burden for them to have to look after and adjust their own lives to.

Ring, ring, ring ... with every ring I tried to think how to tell him what had happened, how I thought this was actually going to stay, it wasn't just going to go away. He answered. I put on my smile and my humour and filled him in, laughing away like it was nothing as tears stream down my face.

When Lee walked through the door, his eyes went straight to me with a look of worry and concern, quickly replaced by humour as he approached me on the floor where I was propped against the island. I was now looking haggard and puffy faced from all the crying that had followed after I'd hung up. As my eyes met his we laughed, because that is what we did, we made fun of each other in the worst of times because neither of us knew how to deal with what was happening and we were both emotionally crippled when it came to expressing emotions.

First, I showed him what happened when I tried to get back up, trying to laugh my way through it. I must have felt I needed to prove I wasn't making it up or overexaggerating. That is when I broke, that is when I allowed myself to show my fear. My body went into full-on shaking, like an epileptic fit; there was no control over my own body which was beyond scary. All the while I was still trying to laugh my way through it because it almost didn't feel real.

Lee scooped me off the floor (real knight in shining armour moment) and carried me as my body still spasmed. He laid me on the sofa, where my whole body spasmed intensely. My muscles would tense, my legs flinging off the sofa and then they'd freeze mid-air. I couldn't relax the muscles to let them come back down to the sofa. Then it was my torso, then both. It was quite a sight to behold. You know in films where they do exorcisms, someone is tied to a bed and their body contorts into all shapes? That's what it was like. There was so much fear yet so much gratitude for having Lee there. I've no idea what he thought about the situation, I think we were both in shock at what he was witnessing and I was experiencing.

That day wasn't just a one-off. Then it got to the point where it was no longer just when I walked, it was when I was sitting, when I was lying down and even when I was sleeping. I couldn't escape it. I didn't even know it was happening when I was sleeping, Lee would tell me in the morning that I'd had a rough night, and I'd think, *Oh, that's why I feel so exhausted and my muscles are already hurting.* We had to call a doctor out.

The doctor came to the house and we explained what had been happening. He seemed a little confused and concerned as it had come out of nowhere in such a short amount of time. I was sent for a scan and that was when I was referred to a neurologist. I also got measured for a wheelchair, and an appointment with an occupational therapist who gave me crutches and a walking frame.

The kids loved the wheelchair: if I wasn't in it, they were. Especially Matthew, who got the hang of pushing himself around and thought it was the best toy ever. He was three.

The next step was to see the neurologist. Again, a moment of hope, someone to explain what was happening to me. I sat in my wheelchair and described what I had been experiencing. She asked me to get up and walk, which I did. It's not an easy thing to explain what this looks like but imagine you're trying to walk with a jackhammer turned on and you're about halfway there.

She told me my scan was normal, just like every other test I had ever had, shocker! The explanation I got was basically 'It's all in your head.' She literally said, with a straight face, 'If you sang a song, it would probably happen less.' With no other explanation other than how my mind would be focused on something else. And as there was nothing showing on the scans there wasn't anything else she could do. Another punch to the stomach! *Why is no one trying to help me? Can't they see how much I'm hurting, how much my life is affected and how much I'm trying to get help? I'm not this 'lazy girl' who wants everything handed to her.*

I would love to say I then proceeded to lose my shit and spill all the depressive, angry, frustrated thoughts that were constantly floating around my head. However, I didn't know how to express myself, I didn't know how to say 'This is not OK'. I was taught the following while growing up: doctors know best; you can't talk back to an authority figure; respect your elders; you must smile and be polite even if you disagree; do not cause others discomfort or make a scene. So, I just thanked her and left. Yes, I thanked her!

I was so fucking angry: how dare she say I was making it up, that singing a song would probably let me walk better. (I tried it, by the way, it was an absolute failure if you're wondering). Although, I did notice the weirdest thing one day: if I lifted my knee up towards my chest like I was doing high knees in slow motion then I could walk better, but no one wants to walk around like they're doing high knees all the time. Plus, when I stopped the tremors came back anyway and it also used more energy to lift my legs in this way than to crawl. I showed my occupational therapist at the time and he couldn't believe what he was seeing. His face was a picture though. It the small things that make my day.

This one moment with the neurologist closed me off from listening to anything to do with the mind because all I heard was *It's all in my head, so I'm just making everything up.*

WHAT WOULD HAVE HELPED

I wanted to be really seen and heard. To have someone carve time out for me, to say 'I see you struggling, I see you fighting and I want to help you if I can.' I'm not asking for doctors to become obsessed with each patient until they are 'cured', I'm just asking for some common human decency. If this neurologist had taken the time to explain how the mind works and broken it down into digestible information, it would have made the world of difference to how she made me feel and how I saw myself. Leaving that office sparked a sense that I was making all this up, which would then rear its ugly head in the times I was already feeling down. All she did was make me feel like what I was going through was all my own fault.

Anyone who suffers with M.E./CFS, Fibromyalgia, PoTS, Long Covid and many other chronic illnesses can't take in a lot of information at one time. It becomes overwhelming and you leave appointments feeling exhausted. You can't remember a fucking thing that was said, which then infuriates and stresses you out even more. That's why most of the chapters in this book are short, or divided into sections.

It might sound silly, but a simpler explanation or visual aids to explain things would have been helpful. If I just felt like she was trying, even just a little bit, it would have helped my self-compassion enormously. Instead of feeling like I was a name on a list and wasting people's time.

I wish some doctors could fathom the difficulties we face when going to appointments. How our anxiety and stress levels are raised massively just to get to the appointment. That our bodies and mind are already on high alert, feeling like we are fighting to get to that seat in front of them. Let alone absorbing what is said to us or responding. In that moment we are in survival mode and our ability to take in new information is dramatically reduced. Our thought process slows to the point where we can find it extremely difficult to even find words to form sentences; we forget what we wanted to really say and we withdraw.

For me, I would nod and agree even when I didn't agree because it was so hard to stay sitting, to fight the stabbing pains while also trying to have a conversation with someone who didn't seem interested or didn't understand what I was experiencing. The anxiety would be so bad I'd feel uncomfortable in my own skin and have this overwhelming feeling of needing to get out.

If the neurologist had explained that there's a blueprint, a map to how your mind works and it's intricately connected to the body and that sometimes the information (a message) gets sent to the body from the mind because it's a message that has been sent before in the past in a similar situation, and can go as far back as childhood. That these messages over time have led to the development of symptoms arising. All this happens unconsciously, on a level in your mind that you're not currently aware of. The symptoms are a way to inform you that there is something in you that needs to be addressed. They are an invitation for the conscious mind to look deeper into the unconscious mind so those messages can stop being sent.

If she'd explained all this, that would have been a great start.

Then I would have known that there's a message (or messages) stuck on a loop that is automatically sent, reinforcing unhelpful beliefs. I would have understood how this wasn't my fault and then maybe, just maybe, I could have understood myself a lot better, a lot earlier.

The beliefs you create as a child are created as a way to survive the environment you had to grow up in and from the conditioning that was passed down to you from your caregivers. As a child you have nowhere else to go but the home you are brought up in. If that home is volatile and you feel unsafe, your mind will adapt ways you can survive that situation. You may energetically scope the room out to see what mood your caregiver is in. You may become the parent and take on responsibilities of the house, so there is less for them to do, in the hopes they will be happier or less stressed so they won't take it out on you or may even have more time for you.

There are many survival mechanisms created in childhood, which you then take with you into adulthood. You are likely unaware of many of the survival strategies you use because they are so engrained into you that they happen at the unconscious level. A program created in your mind to protect you.

By the time you reach the age of seven you have already created your values and beliefs about yourself, others and the world around you. Over those seven years you have absorbed all that is around you like a sponge. This is known as the 'imprint period', or you can think of it like software being installed, just like a computer. These experiences through the imprint years created a program which will automatically run when triggered, leading to pre-programmed behaviours and actions, unless you make a conscious choice to change and build your self-awareness. What I'm trying to say is you are basically running on outdated programs – or as you already know I like to call them ... *lies!*

Your personality is formed by significant emotional events that have occurred in your life before the age of ten. This is where you will have learnt how to model love, relationships, self-worth; anything that has been unprocessed can be carried as shame, guilt, anger, fear etc. These become your stories and they create a filter in which you perceive the world.

For example, if 'love' has only ever been demonstrated as shouting at each other, silent treatment or even abuse then that is your 'normal'. If you then enter a relationship when you're older and there are arguments, silent treatment or abuse then your mind tells you that this is 'love' because you have not been shown anything different. You believe this is what you deserve, that this is what everyone experiences, so you stay.

You do not see these thoughts as something separate from you, even though they are. You take them on as a truth of who you are, the 'I am', the 'this is me' aspect of the mind because the ego takes everything personally.

CHAPTER 10

Nutritional Supplements

Something's happening

After the neurologist appointment around 2014, I withdrew from the world even more. It reinforced the hopelessness I was already feeling and I fell into a deep depression for months. I rarely left the house. When I did, I'd have extreme anxiety unless I was with someone.

And yet, somehow, it was during this bout of depression that I had my 'destined for more' moment that I described at the start of this book. This is when I began to change, I was moving out of victimhood and into something new ... hope! I felt that light burning inside me once again, only small, but that was all I needed to begin making a change.

I had already been stalking a lady on social media who had the same chronic illness as me, the same symptoms, who was also a mum, and was running her own memory blanket business. I'd run my own business making sterling silver jewellery for about three or four years until the tremors made it nearly impossible to carry on with.

I watched this lady for a good month, maybe longer, until I joined her M.E. group on Facebook ... I know, proper stalker vibes! When I saw how she was not just feeling better but actually physically better just by taking some dried fruits and vegetables in a capsule and changing her diet, I thought, *Fuck it, I'll give anything a go.* This lady, Salli, went on to become my best friend, my 'wifey'. If you too would like to stalk her, you can find her as Salli Maddalo on most social media sites. We have been through so much together and our humour matches on a soul level: we can rip the shit out of each other or we can cry until there are no more tears left, sometimes there's no in-between. Don't you just love how the universe works when you just say 'Fuck it! Let's see what happens?'

When I started the supplements all I wanted was a little more energy so I could feel like a mum again. That was it, that was all I wanted. At this time, I barely functioned; I spent my whole day trying not to use any energy so I could make it through the evenings with the kids. I had to feed them, talk to them, maybe play with them if it was a good day, but mostly we watched TV together.

When I try to recall this time of my life it's like my kids didn't exist, there are hardly any memories. Luckily, I have pictures that remind me that I was there with them, I didn't just disappear from their lives – well, maybe not physically but I feel I did mentally and emotionally. I was constantly dissociating, checking out from reality, so now it feels like there was no connection with anyone through that time.

I didn't have high expectations with taking the supplements. The Holland and Barrett vitamins I mentioned taking (chapter 7) didn't seem to do much, I stopped taking them after a few months. Which is why I didn't expect anything to happen overnight with these new supplements. I was prepared to wait a few months before noticing if I felt any better because I knew since it had taken years to get to this point, it would take a long time to see any results. Oh, how wrong I was. Within just a week I noticed I was feeling more present, less foggy. I was interacting with the kids and talking to Lee more. In time, my energy levels improved so much more, the brain fog reduced, my pain was less and my tremors reduced a bit too! I couldn't believe it. It felt too good to be true.

Surely it couldn't be that fucking simple … why had no one told me about the power of food before?! We could be helping so many people if they knew!

This was the starting point of my journey, my turning point, my first step of breaking that limiting belief that told me there was no better life out there for me. No, not any more: after my 'destined for more' moment something changed in me. This is when I found a desire, a want to not just survive but to live, to thrive. It's funny now because I had no idea just how much that one decision to change something in my life would take me on a journey to be fully healed, and to also help others like me. It was a step towards opening up my mind in ways I didn't even think were possible.

I ended up joining the network marketing company (Juice Plus+) where I'd had the supplements from. This turned out to be the best decision I could have made for my mental health and I made friends who have stayed with me until this day.

I even went to Marbella with the company, despite only being with them a few months. I was in such a fuck it! mentality that I decided to say yes when Salli asked if I wanted to go, saying I could travel with her. Bearing in mind I had never met Salli in person, I had extreme anxiety, hardly ever left my house and at this point I was in and out of a wheelchair like a fucking yo-yo.

I couldn't believe I did it, I wouldn't have let myself believe that this was a possibility just a few months earlier. It definitely helped that Salli made me feel safe, that she had my back and that she understood what could happen to me with fatigue, pain and tremors, and that if I was in the wheelchair, I'd need a chauffeur. She was game – who doesn't love a bit of queue jumping?

I became obsessed with learning more about the body and the effect nutrition has on it, not for validation, not to help others, but for me. I wanted to learn all I could about this subject so I could simply help myself. There was finally something I could actively do for myself. I did a nutritional therapy course and other smaller courses and masterclasses so I could learn all that I could to understand my body better.

At this point, my pain was nearly non-existent, but all that had changed was my taking the supplements and switching my diet to a wholefood-based diet. I don't live as intensely by this diet now. I really wish I did but with picky eaters at home (the husband) it was a challenge to make everyone happy. However, I still do about 70 per cent wholefood and 30 per cent whatever I want. I learnt it was about balance and finding what works for you.

My kids also picked up some good habits when I overhauled my diet and they still love veggie sticks, fruit and making food from scratch with me or even by themselves now that they are older. However, it's often the case that people don't want to put the effort in to change their diet. It can seem like too much of an effort or like it's a fad diet – but it's not a diet, it's a way of life, eliminating or reducing processed foods that our bodies can't deal with. So many foods we consume are foreign to our body, going against our natural process to be able to digest these man-made ingredients.

I was shocked that there was so much evidence behind the links between the gut's nervous system – the enteric nervous system – and autoimmune illnesses. How could diet alone make such an improvement, sometimes mitigate symptoms entirely, yet doctors weren't telling patients this? Because they're not taught it. They don't know themselves how changes in diet can improve patient's lives more than medications.

CHAPTER 11

Counselling

Lying to myself

Throughout those positive moments in the previous chapter, however, I was still suffering with severe depression. It came on after seeing the neurologist. I withdrew into myself even more, becoming a shell of myself, feeling so numb and helpless. I discovered a part of the depression was to do with having the coil, so once I had that out, things definitely improved, but I was still struggling so much that I made a very rare doctor's appointment to talk about how I was feeling. This was a few months after the breakthrough moment I described at the very start of the book. Although I had that moment of hope and subsequent action which made me feel physically better through the networking group, I was still feeling very low.

    The doctor I saw wanted to put me on antidepressants and I refused. I'd been on them for postnatal depression after having my daughter and they'd made me fucking useless ... and since I was already pretty useless before taking them I became a ghost of myself on them, like a zombie. The doctor continued to try and convince me and said that one in four people I passed on the street were on citalopram.

    I stood my ground in what I wanted for a change and finally he agreed for me to try counselling. I was open to trying anything that didn't involve taking medication and I am so glad I did the counselling. Don't get me wrong, there is nothing wrong with taking antidepressants, there is a time and place for medication. I did, in fact, go on them years later. I was just at a point where I wanted to try something different; I wanted something more. I wanted to be an active participant in my own healing.

I was so nervous before my first session. I had no idea what to expect. I was in the wheelchair so Lee took me in. We sat in the waiting room of the doctor's surgery, where the counsellor held his sessions. The waiting made my anxiety worse and when I was finally called my heart began pounding so hard. Lee wheeled me into this small, clinically white room as I was so fatigued I couldn't wheel myself, it was a struggle to hold my head up on its own. Most days at this point I was sitting supported with cushions behind my head so I didn't have to use as much energy. Who knew holding your own head up could be so exhausting.

The counsellor smelt of cigarettes, he looked tired and a bit withdrawn, like he'd been through his own shit in life. He seemed nice enough though, as he introduced himself and gave me a rundown of how the sessions would work. I felt such a conflict and range of emotions. I immediately felt so tense sitting there, because having the counselling session at the doctor's surgery just made it feel like I was going to one of my doctor's appointments, which never made me feel good. The counsellor seemed like the first person who actually wanted to know how I was doing, even though I knew it was his job to ask such questions. Nevertheless, I felt seen. But then that itself was an entirely new sensation, which also meant it felt uncomfortable as I wasn't used to this. So – as I always do – I put a smile on my face and out came the humour.

From that first session I mostly remember bright lights and awkward questions I didn't know how to answer. I knew I was supposed to be truthful but there was a niggling voice saying 'It's not safe.' I felt so incredibly tense the entire time. I wish I had been more honest and open, but I just didn't know how.

My default setting, the filter through which I saw the world, was judgement. I always felt judged by others, I was terrible at judging others too, but I was an even harder judge of myself. This is because that is what had been modelled to me when I was younger.

When I say I wish I had been more open I mean things like saying 'Yes' when he asked if I had ever self-harmed, saying 'Yes' to having suicidal thoughts, and not shutting him down when he mentioned my dad. It had been brought up every time I saw a health professional, so I was fed up with everyone telling me that all of it was connected to him and the affair. I was talking to my dad again at this point: we were on really good terms. I didn't want to go backwards. I realised years later that I was being protective of him too. Also, I'd worked too hard to put that shit in a box so I'd never have to bring it up and I could just move on. Sweeping it under the proverbial rug and pretending like nothing ever happened, just like all those years when we were all living under the same roof. The crazy part is, it worked. Well, at least I thought it had. I didn't feel the anger and hatred I once did so that was a good sign, right?! But the truth is I'd tricked myself into believing everything was OK. Why? Because it was the only way I knew how to survive – it was a coping mechanism.

I turned up to my counselling session every week for six weeks. By the end it was quite nice having someone to talk to. I still struggled to say what I was truly thinking and feeling but I wasn't as tense as those first few sessions. It was progress, another turning point.

The sessions really helped me to realise that I was in fact in denial about accepting this illness. What I really believed under the persona I showed the world and even myself was I believed myself to *be* M.E., that it was my identity, it wasn't separate from me, it was all of me, consuming me. I believed that there was nothing else to me. It was all I could see. It came before everything. Before being a mum, a wife, a business owner because I first had to check my levels to see what I had available for my children, my husband and my business.

I'll never forget when the counsellor said I was the most positive person he'd ever met with M.E. and he couldn't believe how positive I was through everything I had been through and was still experiencing. He told me I was an 'inspiration' and that I could be a 'beacon of light for others'. At the time it gave me confidence and also led me to share my story with others. However, now I know I was just that good at pretending that I fooled him into believing my false persona too.

At some point in the penultimate session we realised that my body was in a constant state of tension and it was that tension that was causing the tremors and spasms to intensify. It was just so normal to me at that point that I didn't realise I was doing it and I didn't know how to switch it off. I practised relaxing my legs consciously during the session, which took a lot of mental concentration as I closed my eyes, moved from the top of my body down, focusing on my breath – just as I did in the final hundred metres during a race. I had to learn this technique as my legs use to tighten up the closer I got to the finish line but I knew I could do better if I could learn to relax at the same time as giving more.

We then continued the session as normal and after a few minutes we checked in to see how my body was doing. Every time my muscles had become tense again and my whole body was locking up. To me, though, it just felt normal; this was my relaxed state, I thought. My default setting wasn't to relax, it was to tense. To constantly be on alert, constantly using energy, to be ready to fight or fly. I was in a constant state of stress. So much so my body (and my nervous system, as I'd later find out) was retuning itself.

My body was not self-regulating, it wasn't coming back to homeostasis, a place of stability and calm. Instead, it was being retriggered by more stress on the system, so my body wasn't finding safety, which is essential for homeostasis. Over time, my system began to adapt to this constant stress, gradually perceiving non-threatening or stressful situations as threatening. The stress levels weren't returning back to that place of calm and safety before being introduced to more perceived stress. This meant I was constantly 'stuck' in fight or flight, unable to relax and repair.

The difficult fact about facing the truth is that it can be triggering; it can open a door for more negative thoughts to swarm in. Fear can begin to spiral and if you don't have the tools, techniques or someone to help you move through this it can be much harder to deal with and make progress. It's why talk therapy can be triggering for some. This is what I found happened to me.

My counselling sessions ran for six weeks. About a month or so after the sessions came to an end I realised that I had opened something up in myself through the sessions and I probably needed another six sessions to understand what had been unleashed. After those sessions, I was back to only having myself to talk to and no clue how to help myself. I hadn't been taught any tools or techniques to help me cope moving forward. When I think about it now, it was a pretty abrupt finish as there really was no aftercare, no additional support, just 'Well that's the last session, it was nice to meet you and good luck with everything moving forward.'

During the next half-term break I found myself hiding from the kids behind the kitchen island, in a desperate need of escape. I needed everything to just stop. I sat there and cried and cried, not knowing how to do this, to live, to be a mum, to keep them alive when I could barely keep myself alive. And yet all I could hear were my kids in the background playing and laughing.

I felt so alone. I no longer knew who I was. I'd admitted in my sessions that I believed myself to *be* M.E., but if by the end of the sessions I knew this wasn't true then who was I if I wasn't this illness? Everything felt like a lie and I didn't know how to move forward.

My old friend was back, joining me in the darkness of the nights as I lay wide awake, trying to fight the tremors. The familiar voice of *This is it for you, there is nothing else, stop trying to be something you're not, you're nothing, you're a burden to him, your kids hate you for not taking them to parties and doing what their friends are doing. How could you think you could have more? You're so greedy.*

There was one night when all I wanted to do was take every tablet in the house. I was done, I was ready for it all to stop now, I hurt too much, I was exhausted. I was so exhausted from all the tremors that

I didn't know how to move. But the tablets were downstairs in the kitchen. The next morning, I could barely lift my head off the pillow. I was so drained that Lee had to dress me and carry me downstairs. I never mentioned a word of how ready I was to leave this world, how I felt like such a burden in his life.

The thought of it now, knowing Lee would have woken up to me unresponsive next to him just fills me with so much guilt and shame. But that is the reality of depression, of being so low, and feeling so much emotionally and physically that you just want it to stop. When you are surrounded by the midst of despair, there is no logic, understanding, or empathy for others. It is only you, your mind and your pain that you can hear.

In hindsight I should have found a private counsellor or coach to help with the next steps but I was just so lost and detached that I didn't know what I needed and I would always tell myself I couldn't afford it. The truth is, I could have if I really tried or I could have asked for help, but I'm sure you're aware by now that I wasn't exactly great with using my words, let alone asking for something from someone. And in all honesty, I didn't know I needed help. Well, I did, I just didn't believe anyone could help me. All I knew was the last help (the counsellor) I had, had made me worse. Not that I was thinking about this consciously, it was more of an unconscious belief, therefore I needed to keep myself safe in what I already knew.

At some point I also saw a psychotherapist and psychiatrist. It's all a bit of a blur and I can only remember bits and pieces. I must have been referred to them by the neurologist (you know, because everything was in my head). This may have even been before I saw the counsellor.

The fact that it is such a blur and I was so detached from myself when all that happened makes me think it must have been before the counselling sessions. If this is the case, then I would have seen the psychologist and psychiatrist at some point in 2014 or 2015.

I think it was the psychiatrist who saw me for a consultation and asked me question after question. Any time my dad was mentioned I would get defensive, as if I had to protect him. I downplayed what I felt or just didn't answer the question truthfully at all. When the session came to an end she said there was no need for me to see her again. She thought I was doing well considering my circumstances.

Even though I saw the psychologist for a few weeks, I couldn't tell you much about it, other than sitting in an uncomfortable chair, in a somewhat dark and plain room. I was directly opposite her with a small table between us. I was so dissociated at this time, so numb, that there are no specifics I can recall about any of the sessions other than crying. There was a lot of crying. I know we spoke about Dad because all my paperwork referenced the affair as the point when everything started.

The psychologist must have understood this was the root cause, that it was this traumatic experience that had led to what I was now experiencing but no one took the time to actually tell me this, to explain how this was a normal response to trauma and that I was in a constant state of survival mode as there were so many unprocessed life experiences that were being retriggered over and over again.

No, instead, we just talked and talked and talked but I still left with the tremors, I was still in and out of the wheelchair and I always left feeling completely and utterly drained, emotionally. I was existing, not living, only just able to speak some days; I'd form sentences thinking I was talking coherently but my sentences wouldn't actually make any sense at all, or I'd believe I was an active participant in conversations only to realise I'd said everything in my head, none of it had ever left my mouth.

I felt like a ghost. Like no one really saw me and I was just floating above my body watching my life. I was living in such an automatic state of being that I was no longer making conscious decisions. Everything was being run by my unconscious mind. A way to protect me further. It was like I was a robot. I just remember feeling so numb. Feeling utterly useless and pointless being in the world, once again.

I was still taking the supplements but I was beginning to question if they were even working any more. So I decided to stop taking them to see if I was right. I was wrong, very wrong. My symptoms got much worse when I did, especially the tremors, so I started them again. It was quite nice knowing it could be worse, that I was doing something to help. It might not be giving me the results I wanted but it was better.

In the next chapter, I share possibly the most important piece of knowledge that was missing throughout this lowest point in my life. I don't want you to go through what I went through, so get ready to master how all of this is linked to the nervous system's response to trauma. Take your time reading it. Come back to it as many times as you need to and respect your energy levels, have a break if you need to.

CHAPTER 12

The Nervous System

Finally, something that makes sense

Trauma is not what happen to you but what happened inside of you as a result of what happened to you. Basically, it is an internal experience not the external event itself. It's why everyone is affected differently by the same event. Those who were unable to resolve the experience store it in the mind and body, which can also affect the spirit, because, say it with me ... they're all connected!

Trauma isn't just an external event; it's actually encoded within our nervous system. Surprising, right? We tend to think of a trauma as something that happened *to* us, like accidents, abuse, or painful memories, but the truth is it lives *inside* us. It is not the event itself that lingers but the imprint it leaves behind in your nervous system, which connects to both the mind and body. When the original event occurred you experienced certain bodily sensations, which generate specific thoughts and beliefs. These thoughts and beliefs often loop in your mind, triggered by certain cues, and linger long after the event has passed. The trauma becomes stored in your mind and body until you're ready to confront it, process it, and uncover the truth that lies behind it.

The nervous system

Let's take a closer look at the nervous system and break it down.

- autonomic nervous system (ANS)
- parasympathetic nervous system (PSNS)
- enteric nervous system (ENS)
- peripheral nervous system (PNS)
- somatic nervous system
- sympathetic nervous system (SNS)

Your nervous system is your body's command centre. Think of it as the ultimate boss of your body – it's in charge of everything from moving to thinking to handling things you're not even aware of. It regulates and directs all movement, thought, and the unconscious mind. The nervous system transmits electrical signals, known as nerve impulses, between different parts of the body and is divided into two systems: the brainy central nervous system (CNS) with the brain and spinal cord, and the outreaching peripheral nervous system (PNS) that hooks everything up to the rest of you. Picture the PNS like a network of tree roots spreading out.

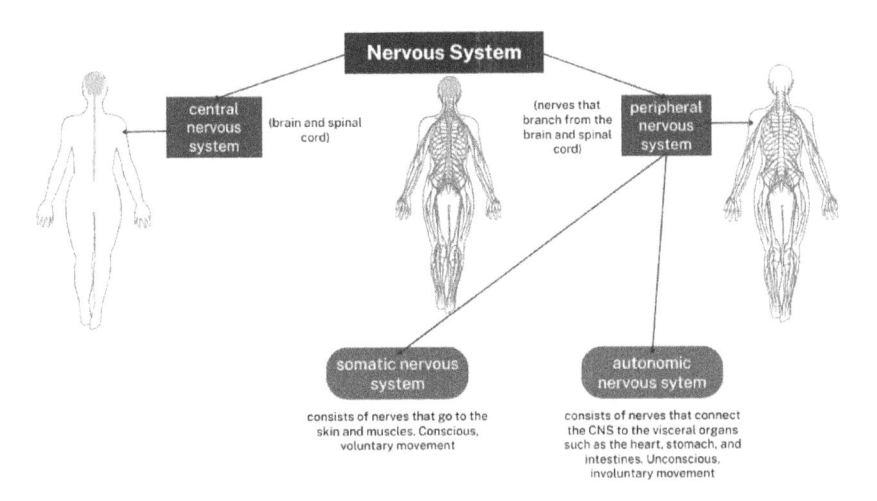

Figure 2. The nervous system

The PNS can be divided again between the somatic nervous system and the autonomic nervous system (ANS). Now, let's zoom in on the autonomic nervous system (ANS) within the peripheral nervous system (PNS). The ANS handles all sorts of automatic functions like breathing, heart rate, and digestion. And guess what? It's not just one big system; it's actually split into three smaller teams: the sympathetic nervous system (SNS), the enteric nervous system (ENS), and the parasympathetic nervous system (PSNS). Each of these squads has its own specific tasks to keep your body running smoothly.

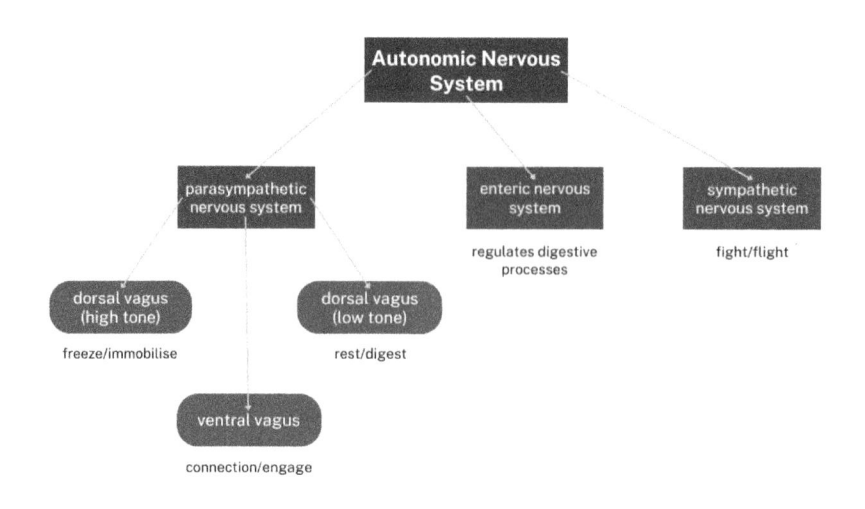

Figure 3. Autonomic nervous system

SYMPATHETIC NERVOUS SYSTEM (SNS)

The SNS is activated during an emergency: the fight-or-flight response. It is a whole-body response, initiating an increase in the flow of oxygenated and nutrient-rich blood to your skeletal muscles, leading to increased heart rate.[7] Of course, this was essential back in the day when it was a fight for survival and those sabre-toothed tigers were lurking around. Now it's more of an internal battle with our own thoughts and the pressure we put on ourselves or feel from society.

Although there are a number of things that affect this system, what we are seeing more and more is that chronic stress, anxiety and trauma cause the SNS to switch on more frequently. The problem comes when you are not fully recovering from any stress or trauma and your nervous system begins to retune itself to this ongoing activation, which can cause nervousness, anxiety or a feeling of being wound up, where your body is constantly feeling tense.

Stress can be good for you as it can make you more resilient when it comes to challenges, but only when you have the chance to recover.

During periods of stress your SNS switch activates. A normally regulated nervous system experiences stress and then returns to normal when the threat has passed. This happens regularly throughout the day: if you're running late, your SNS activates and then once you arrive you begin to settle and your PSNS activates, completing the stress loop. It is constantly fluctuating, a bit like a dance. This is your body's natural ability to self-regulate, referred to as the 'window of tolerance'. These everyday experiences are not perceived as traumatic or fundamentally dangerous, they are just the ebb and flow of life. Unfortunately, if you are 'stuck' in the SNS your body can't rest, recover or repair, which means you can't heal.

Traumatic events push you right out of the window of tolerance and you lose your ability to self-regulate. You may find that you become stuck in this activated SNS – known as hyperarousal – which can make you feel emotionally flooded, reactive, impulsive, hypervigilant, fearful, angry. As well as having intrusive imagery and its effects: racing thoughts, flashbacks, nightmares, high-risk behaviour.[8] The physical state of this hyperarousal is stressful for every system in the body.

Or you may find that you become stuck in PSNS – known as hypoarousal – which is a state of submission or freeze response, leading to feeling numb, empty or dead. Common responses include cognitively dissociating, an inability to think, having collapsed, disabled defensive responses and a sense of helplessness and hopelessness, leading to depression. An effort to reduce this state may include suicide planning, self-harm, compulsive cleaning, or abuse of alcohol or opiates.

You can alternate between these highs and lows. Knowing the language of your body allows you to recognise when you are being pulled out of balance and becoming stuck in either the SNS or PSNS.

PARASYMPATHETIC NERVOUS SYSTEM (PSNS)

The PSNS is commonly known for regulating the rest and digest response. It swings into action during periods of safety, conserving energy essential for fundamental bodily functions such as digestion, urination and reproduction. It also slows your breathing and heart rate. However, the PSNS can actually be divided further based on a specific nerve called the vagus nerve.

The vagus nerve is part of the PSNS, which calms your body after you've been in a stressful situation. It establishes one of the connections between the brain and the gastrointestinal tract and sends information about the state of the inner organs to the brain.[9] Imagine the vagus nerve as this mega highway linking your brain and body – it's like the ultimate communication superhighway. It's the hotline for info about how your organs are doing, making sure everything's running smoothly.

Here's the cool part: this nerve is mostly about listening. About 80 percent of it is all about sending messages from your body to your brain, while the other 20 percent does the opposite, carrying signals from your brain back to your body. So, while we often focus on mental health strategies targeting the brain, it's just as crucial to tune into what your body's telling you. Your body's got a lot to say, so listening in can really help you stay balanced and healthy.

20% is motor information being sent from the brain to the body

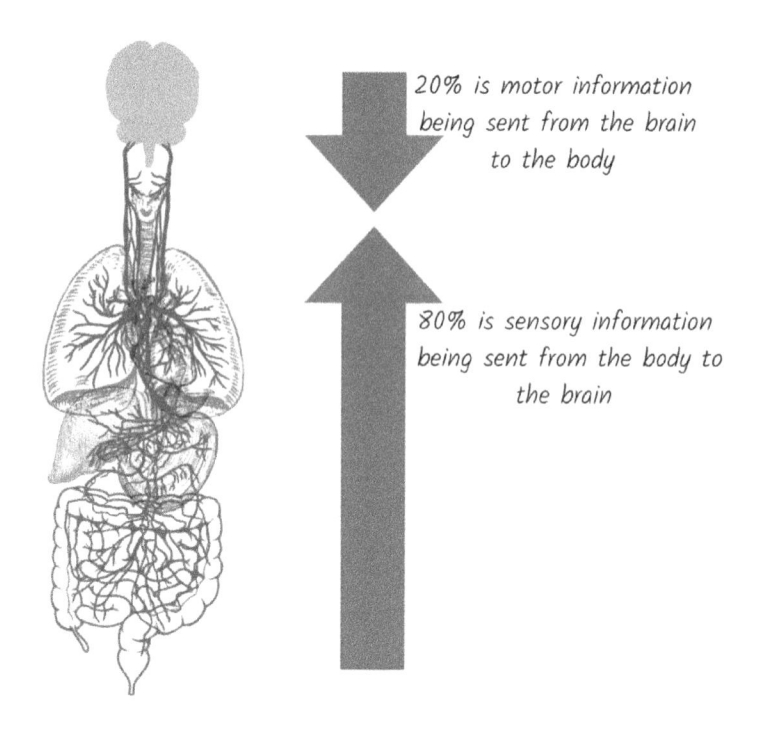

80% is sensory information being sent from the body to the brain

Figure 4. Information being sent to and from the brain, via the vagus nerve

In my opinion, this shows why it is so important to work with the body just as much as the mind – actually, even more so. I want you to think of a time you got scared or frightened, take a moment to really bring that time up in your mind. Right now, as you recall it, do you notice how you first *felt* the fear before you could think you were scared? Maybe you noticed your heart rate increased, your mouth went dry, you felt tension in your stomach or legs. That is because your body reacts first, then you begin to filter the experience based on your previous experiences. If you had a childhood where you were abused or were constantly walking on eggshells your reaction could trigger a panic attack. Contrarily, someone who doesn't have the same trigger can process the sense of fear and self-regulate back to homeostasis, whereas you may feel the effects of that fright for minutes, hours, or even days.

The vagus nerve has two branches, which both serve as a central function in allowing your body to achieve homeostasis. But overactivation of either system (SNS, stress response; PSNS, calming response) is not beneficial for your wellbeing.

Understanding the different aspects of the vagus nerve helps explain the shutdown response that is very common in chronic illness patients.

Ventral vagus – connection, engagement
When this is activated you feel safe; it is why we crave connection. Social interaction can stimulate the PNS to feel safe.

If you have difficulties with feeling safe or forming connections it can be linked to insufficient activation of the ventral vagus, particularly during childhood, which can impact one's ability to regulate emotions and respond to stress effectively.

Dorsal vagus (low tone) – rest, digest
This is what we know as the PSNS: the calming, homeostasis state. When this aspect of the vagus nerve is active, it promotes a sense of calm and balance. Fear takes a back seat, and you're left feeling safe. Plus, your blood flow shifts to support digestion and other important bodily functions, not just your limbs.

Dorsal vagus (high tone) – freeze, immobilisation

Constant or too much activation of this nerve causes you to dissociate and become immobile. When this nerve goes into overdrive, you might find yourself zoning out or feeling totally stuck. It can mess with your ability to think straight or get your words out right.

So, you see, you are not broken, you do not need fixing; there is a reason, a blueprint to who you are. Right now, you're just dealing with the aftermath of trauma and the beliefs it's left behind. These beliefs often revolve around feeling unsafe, unworthy, or inadequate.

Now that you're aware of this, how do you start the healing process? It's about learning to soothe and regulate your nervous system while also delving into the root cause of the trauma.

AN IMBALANCED NERVOUS SYSTEM

There is such a thing called 'dysautonomia' which is a condition characterized by an imbalance in the autonomic nervous system (ANS). It's a medical term used to describe when the ANS isn't functioning properly. The list of symptoms looks like this:

- Fatigue
- Sleep disruptions – insomnia, unrefreshing sleep
- Orthostatic intolerance – symptoms become worse when standing
- Cognitive impairment – brain fog, memory problems, poor concentration, difficulty retrieving or forming words
- Pain
- Cold hands and feet
- Heart palpitations
- Stress-related symptoms – anxiety, panic, heart palpitations, difficulty tolerating stress
- Headaches – of a new type, pattern or severity
- Nausea
- Increased sensitivity
- Gastrointestinal issues

Look familiar? It should do as it is near enough the same symptoms of M.E./CFS and other chronic illnesses. However, the symptoms are not the issue, the root causes leading to the symptoms is the issue that needs addressing.

TECHNIQUES FOR SOOTHING THE NERVOUS SYSTEM

Here are some super simple soothing techniques you can do at any time – and the best part is you can start using them right away. This is because they are soothing techniques, helping to guide your body back into the PSNS.

These techniques are not to 'heal' or 'cure' you but they can open a door back to calm and it is from that place that you can begin to investigate and get curious as to why you are experiencing certain symptoms.

If we use the analogy of being in a tornado then I'm sure you can imagine the chaos, things swirling around, not being able to think or see properly, but using some simple techniques will guide you to the eye of the storm. Where it is quiet and calm. You can think. From there you can work on different things to help the tornado dissipate, or to find a path through it … because yes, you have the ability to do that.

Soothing nervous system techniques
1. **Humming (I know, ironic seeing as the neurologist told me to sing and I rolled my eyes at it!)**
- That's it, it's that simple: hum
- Keep your lips together and breathe in and out through your nose

- Trust yourself to hum in a way that is right for you, that calms you; whether it is a song, a single note or something in-between
- Play around and find what soothes you best; you'll know it's working when you feel calmer than when you started
- This stimulates the vagus nerve, allowing you to switch on the PSNS, finding a place of safety

2. **Heartbeat tap**
- Begin with your hand over your heart – palm flat
- Start tapping a heartbeat pattern – 'du-dum' – matching your current rhythm (so it may be fast to start with)
- Then begin to slow the rhythm until you feel more at ease
- Notice your breath and allow it slow; expand your diaphragm more with each breath
- Do this for as long as you need

3. **Box breathing**
- Sit up straight, get comfortable
- Lift your shoulders to your ears as you inhale
- Drop your shoulders on an exhale, noticing how they relax
- Now breathe in through your nose for a count of 4
- Hold the breath for a count of 4
- Exhale through your nose for a count of 4 and then hold your breath again for a count of 4
- Then repeat the process

- If it's new and uncomfortable for you, start with a few rounds, then build up to a few minutes
- Finish by allowing your breathing to come back to normal and sit for a few minutes, allowing your mind to wander where it wishes but not becoming fixated on whatever arises

Follow along with these practices at www.hope-light.co.uk/bookresources.

CHAPTER 13

Trauma And The Nervous System

The real cause

Trauma – Greek origin meaning 'wound'

We all have wounds. Some are bigger than others, some run deeper than others. Everyone has suffered trauma in some way. That trauma has then gone on to dictate how you cope, how you behave, how you react and even how you think.

It is now my belief that chronic illnesses are caused by an event/s in our lives that left us wounded; our life experiences that have been held within, unprocessed for years. I have seen it time and time again with my clients. There is *always* a root cause that has led to the expression of the illness.

When you have a cut on your arm (a wound), you can see it. You know it is there. Sometimes, you don't know you have a cut and then once you see it, it suddenly hurts. Once you do see it, you can aid in its healing by cleaning it, adding a plaster, and creating a safe environment for it to heal.

The same thing can happen with emotional wounds. You don't always know they are there, but once you have an awareness of them, they can start to hurt, feel painful and in that moment, you can choose to create an environment to heal them or you can choose to leave them and let them scar – becoming numb to your own feelings.

You already have the ability to self-heal: you know this, you don't consciously tell your arm to heal, it's a natural process. It's similar when it comes to emotional wounds, except that in order to foster the right environment for healing, you need to take accountability – taking action such as changing your diet or seeking a professional trained to help you navigate your emotions and unprocessed events in a space you deem safe. Emotional healing is also a choice because most of us weren't brought up in an environment that taught us to self-regulate and know it is safe to have those feelings, specifically the more negative emotions. These wounds – or more specifically, these unprocessed life experiences – cause a disruption in your body and its energetic flow moving forward. Over time, this build-up of multiple wounds leads to physical issues such as fatigue, pain, anxiety, and depression due to the impact it has on the body at a cellular level.

A study found 31 per cent of young people had a traumatic experience during childhood, and those who were exposed to trauma were twice as likely as their peers to have a range of mental health disorders.[10]

About fifteen million people in England have a long-term condition, for which there is currently no cure, such as diabetes, chronic obstructive pulmonary disease, arthritis and hypertension.[11] And more than fourteen million people have two or more health conditions. Analysis of GP data in England suggested hypertension (18.2 per cent), depression/anxiety (10.3 per cent) and chronic pain (10.1 per cent) were the three most common health conditions.[12]

Healing truly is available to everyone. But this belief starts with changing our perspective and to stop looking at an illness as something to be cured by giving medication or even surgeries. Instead, we need to look at illness and disease as a consequence of life, as something unresolved, unhealed. We also need to look at each person as a whole, seeing the mind, body and spirit as one, rather than as separate entities; then there could be so much more healing available for everyone, every day. How incredibly powerful would that be?

Remember, however, you want to *heal* this wound, not stick a plaster on it and pretend it's not there. If you allowed yourself to focus on healing, you would no longer see yourself as broken. Instead, you would reframe your symptoms as an alarm that alerts you to something within you that needs addressing.

Please note, this does not mean stopping any medications, because there are times when medication is needed, times where you have not yet reached the point of accepting help or facing past hurts. Nor does it mean you have to speak for hours each week about your feelings. For some this is great; I needed this for myself to start with and still need to talk for hours at times. However, talking is just one part of the healing process; you also have to allow your body to process it, as your body remembers so much more than you realise. This time for processing allows you to complete the stress loop that never closed, which I describe further on in this chapter.

Yes, facing things that may be uncomfortable or painful can be extremely hard and yes, that may stop you seeking help initially. But let me ask you these questions: would you like to be healed? Would you like a better life? A better mind and body? I'm guessing the answer is 'yes'. Then something has to change. Staying where you are, not facing the traumas, not dealing with unresolved emotions, will only keep that programming running and keep you there, stuck in your own form of suffering, being triggered again and again.

When a trauma happens, we don't consciously think *Ooh, that is too much to process and understand, let's tuck that away to deal with later.* Your mind and body aren't fully aware of what is happening and your need to survive is triggered. Decisions are made based on your nervous system's programming, which is based on what you know about yourself. Ask yourself: are you emotionally equipped? Do you have the mental capacity and energy to deal with this right here, right now?

These are not conscious decisions that you make for yourself, there is something much bigger at play that connects to your mind, body and spirit – remember! they are not separate; they are interwoven, working as one.

Trauma has an invisible scale and everyone's personal trauma scale is unique; you know how much you are able to consciously deal with, whether that is physically, emotionally, mentally or spiritually. It is even based on your age and how developed your brain is. When you are younger you don't have the emotional knowledge to be able to understand what is happening. 'Something' bigger just knows when you are not able to cope, it knows when you don't feel safe and are not equipped physically, emotionally or spiritually to handle whatever has just been thrown at you.

This is what triggers the need to protect yourself, to survive at all costs. In that moment, you're essentially rescuing yourself because deep down, your ego mind fixates on the possibility that the overwhelming influx of pain and emotions could lead to something as serious as death, due to your unconscious programming.

Your survival instinct cannot allow that to happen – and neither can the ego mind as its main priority is to keep you alive. It believes that you would not be alive without it; that it is the very thing that pumps life through your body. But you have to understand that *this is not true*: our bodies are intricate pieces of art with many, many layers, far beyond what we are currently able to comprehend.

From the moment you experience any trauma, your mind and body will decide on the best way to survive, creating coping mechanisms and strategies. If you feel humiliated you may hide behind humour or you take yourself too seriously. If you're unable to emotionally process the event you may withdraw and become numb or detach from your body. Your mind and body's reasoning being if you're numb then you won't have to feel all these emotions that are just too big and all-consuming for you. This is all based on previous experiences from childhood. In this example, you didn't feel safe enough with your caregivers to express yourself, so you learnt it was safer to shut your emotions down. Now as an adult you are unable to speak up when you deeply want to or you may be unable to even identify the specific emotions you are having. That imprint of it not being safe to speak up is retriggered every time you want to speak up and be heard, so you cut yourself off before you even attempt to speak up.

Traumas can even cause you to forget details of the event or the entire event altogether as your unconscious mind takes over to protect you and stores it in the deepest hidden depths of your mind as well as your body, which manifests as one or several dysregulated nervous system symptoms. The prime directive of the unconscious mind is to protect you at all costs and to make sure you survive no matter what.

Trauma is something we all experience to varying degrees. There is no escaping it, so by understanding it and recognising it for what it is, you can begin to find the truth behind what you are living with.

How trauma is created

We've discussed trauma being an unprocessed life experience. But how did it become unprocessed? When you perceive a threat – whether that is physically, emotionally or mentally – you are hardwired to switch to survival mode. The fight, flight, freeze or fawn response starts pumping through your system. I imagine most of you have heard of 'fight, flight, freeze' but not 'fawn'. The best way to explain the fawn response is people-pleasing. It occurs when you try to keep the threat/person happy even if it goes against your beliefs, needs and wants. This response can come about when you have experienced a long period in an emotionally and/or physically abusive environment. You will likely have tried the fight, flight or freeze response first and learnt over time the best way to survive was to please the other person: the fawn response.

During survival mode, messages are sent to your organs to send blood to your limbs so you can fight or run. Once the threat passes you send messages of safety through your system, cortisol levels drop and you come back to your natural state of being, closing the loop.

However, if you do not get the message of safety your system keeps survival mode switched on; the stress loop never completes and you're unable to come back to that natural state of being (homeostasis).

Meaning the whole event never actually stops and continues to live in your unconscious being and is imprinted in your nervous system.

The Stress/Trauma Loop

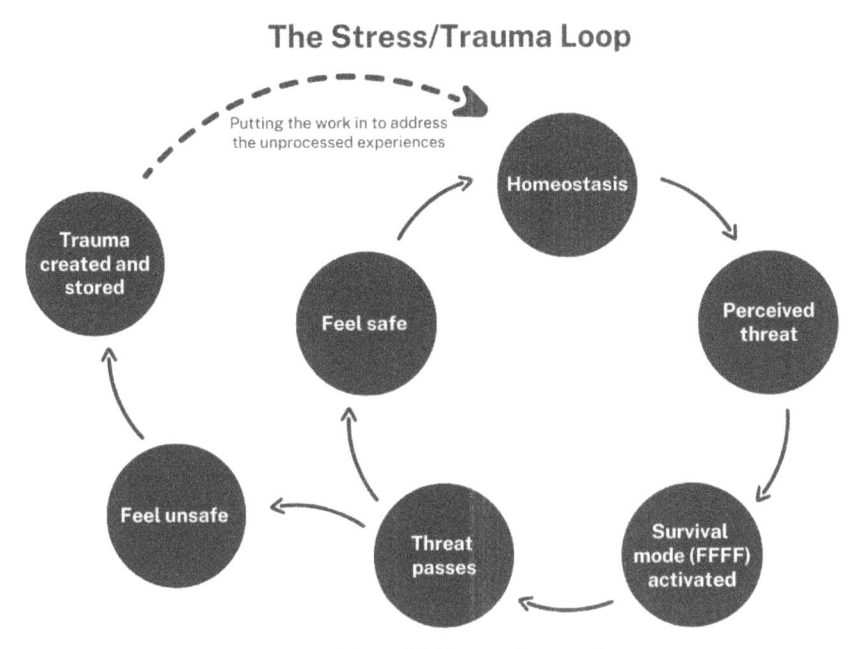

- Homeostasis
- Perceived threat
- Survival mode (FFFF) activated
- Threat passes
- Feel unsafe
- Trauma created and stored
- Putting the work in to address the unprocessed experiences
- Feel safe

Figure 5. The stress/trauma loop

CHAPTER 14

Types Of Traumas

As I mentioned previously, trauma has its own scale – or you could call it a spectrum. The world of trauma healing often refers to 'Big T' traumas and 'little t' traumas. But let's take a closer look through the lens of the nervous system.

I want to make it crystal clear that it does not matter how 'big' or 'small' your trauma is, trauma is trauma. Just because someone has more symptoms or worse symptoms than you, does not mean your experience is any less. Your experience is based on your own ability to handle what you were given at the time.

ACUTE TRAUMA

When most people think of trauma, they immediately think of those unforgettable, single life-changing events. Trauma in the form of a big life-changing event is one that we are consciously aware of because, let's face it, you know when something comes out of left field and smacks you in the face. It's almost too powerful, too much, too overwhelming for you to comprehend, to feel, to process.

This plays into the stress loop I talked about in the previous chapter (figure 5). The event triggers the survival response of the nervous system which is to fight, flight, freeze or fawn. When the survival response doesn't find that completion in the nervous system it begins to show up symptomatically in your mind, creating thoughts and beliefs that support the response your nervous system is still feeling.

The trauma isn't over until the body feels safe and knows it's over.

For me, the acute trauma was not the divorce of my parents but the news of the affair and its aftermath, which included the emotional neglect I felt, plus the inability to understand and comprehend what was going on as my brain had not fully developed enough to be able to process the events. Your brain goes through a fascinating journey of development, with the finishing touches not happening until your mid to late twenties. The last part of the brain to reach maturity is the prefrontal cortex, which is like your brain's CEO – it's in charge of complex decision-making, planning, problem-solving, self-control, and social behaviour. One of the most remarkable aspects of the prefrontal cortex is its ability to regulate emotions and impulses. It helps you resist immediate gratification in favour of long-term goals and enables you to adapt to changing situations by inhibiting inappropriate behaviours. It makes sense now, doesn't it? Why I experienced what I did and why.

I was fifteen when I was told about the affair. I was sixteen when I had glandular fever and I was seventeen when I began getting the persistent, sharp stabbing pains in my head.

At fifteen I was still finalising who I was: my personality, my beliefs. These are all things that are created in childhood and modelled to you by your caregivers. For me that was to always be kind, to be respectful, to do as you're told, to never talk back, never do anything that could be construed as 'wrong' because you will always be found out. I had to be a 'good girl' at all times.

The affair undid all of who I thought I was, who he had drilled into me to be and who I thought he was. I became like a doe caught in headlights, unable to move, unable to understand, to filter the infinite amount of conflicting information that was cascading through my mind and body, setting my nervous system on high alert. Due to not feeling safe during this time my nervous system stayed on high alert, and thus the trauma imprinted and began to live in my mind and body.

The trauma, the internal wound, kept me frozen in time (the freeze response) like my brain was shoved in a freezer left in a dark cold place, unable to move forward. I was left with those thoughts of disbelief and utter confusion constantly swirling around. Left in the darkness with those thoughts, left long enough for them to start to turn to anger, to hurt, to pain, to everything feeling like a complete and utter lie. Like the reality I once lived in no longer existed. I was ripped into a new, unforgiving reality, a new lens through which I saw the world.

But there was nowhere for all this hatred and pain to go, other than to be kept inside this hollow, lonely space. Imprinting in my nervous system. There was no one to speak to, and there were no words that I knew to say to be able to even begin unravelling what was haunting me. So the darkness stayed, becoming so familiar, becoming my only friend. A friend who knew what I thought, how I felt, always there in the shadows, in the nights when I couldn't sleep. Leading me to the drinking and the cutting, as a way to numb, to hide, to escape and to control what I had left.

It was this voice that taught me how to pretend, how to smile, how to joke and mask while still feeling this swirling chaos inside. It was this invisible friend that held my hand as I had to face my parents each day, that helped me keep in my tears and screams.

Those silent screams for help that I desperately wanted my mum to hear, to notice me. The screams of *WHY?!* It was this voice that unconsciously taught me to relax my body when I was around my dad, to be pleasant and kind and to hold my tongue. It was the fawn response. I even tricked myself to think, *Everything is fine, I can make it through this, it's not so bad.* And it really wasn't that bad, it was just how I perceived things internally and the emotions I had now attached to him.

All these coping mechanisms and strategies emerged so I could survive and get through another day. Well, at least until the nights rolled in again and I was in the safety of my room once more. My safe space to let the barrier down, where the thunderous thoughts would roll back in. But now, that friend who had helped me through the days didn't feel like a friend any more ... it felt more like a shadow, a ghost, a nightmare. The nights became a fuel for the anger and pain, a place where chaos reigned, a place where it grew stronger, putting down roots deep inside me. Activating the stress cycle and never reaching completion, therefore embedding the emotional response to the trauma deeper into my psyche and nervous system.

The voice was taunting: *No one cares about you, you're all alone, you're just attention-seeking, nobody cares, nobody cares, nobody cares.*

That is the power of the ego when left unchecked, when those thoughts and feelings are left to run rampant, flooding your mind and body, suffocating you from the inside.

The spark that once drove you becomes dimmer and dimmer. Each day you live like this you give a little more power over to the ego, because trying to fight the ego becomes too hard, and you become exhausted. Bit by bit, you get to a point where you are no longer conscious of what is happening around you; your days become a blur as you start to dissociate. No longer living in the present, only living to survive not to thrive.

DEVELOPMENTAL TRAUMA

'Developmental' or 'attachment' trauma tends to occur between birth and seven years old, as these are the years that lay the foundation for who we become. Some feel developmental trauma originates during the first three years of your life as this is when you are in a place of attachment; you cannot survive without your caregivers. You can experience this later in life, like in a relationship where you experience abuse, a messy divorce or even incarceration. Any extended period of development that lasts longer than a year can shape and influence you, leading to the development of new coping mechanisms as you strive to adapt and survive.

Unconsciously, you see your caregivers as your only source of survival. But maybe your parents have their own trauma and things going on, so they aren't very present with you, leading to you not getting the connection and sense of safety you need. Maybe you cry, feel sad or angry but your parents don't make you feel safe and seen in that moment; maybe they shut you down, telling you *It's not that bad, it could be worse, suck it up.* You learn that your emotions aren't allowed, that they're not spoken about and aren't valid.

Your emotions have now become a threat to your survival, so you push them out. But in doing so, the emotions remain a threat because they still exist. Your relationship with anger and sadness becomes one of resistance, one to avoid. Any time you feel that emotion – anger, for example – rise, a shutdown response activates, as this has now become the trained response (or program) since you were young. This can lead to people walking all over you as an adult because you don't know how to experience healthy anger.

It can also go the opposite way where you were modelled anger as a child and you learnt anger was a good way to deal with the threat at the time. This then wires into your nervous system over and over again until it becomes an automatic response. Then, whenever a perceived threat comes up you default to anger and a fight response because that served you when you were younger.

It can even develop as simply as your parents being unable to connect with you when you were born, like postnatal depression or an absent parent. It instantly becomes an attachment trauma without even realising it. I know this to be true with my daughter. I'll go into this more shortly.

Developmental trauma is connected with those 'little ts'. They can be seemingly insignificant events expressed and experienced so subtly that they mostly go unnoticed. Or it may be such a constant in your life you just don't know any different. When people tell you the same thing over and over again as you grow up, it just becomes normal to you. If you hear from a young age that you are stupid you will find yourself repeating that same phrase to yourself: *Ugh, why did I do that, I'm so stupid!* You will end up using this self-talk without being aware of it because it has created a neural pathway that is now an automatic thought. A constant hum under the everyday chatter.

For me, understanding this type of trauma helped me to understand some of my behaviours and actions. When I first started doing work on finding the cause of things, at times I would get frustrated because I couldn't pinpoint when or what was the cause, so I felt like I was in limbo: trying to heal but not knowing where to look.

I learnt that the signs of developmental trauma are things like saying your childhood was good, nothing went wrong and idealising your childhood, which is me all over! I even start this book by saying this: "My childhood growing up was a pretty normal and standard one." Other symptoms are dissociation (when you're not completely present), shutting down emotions, emotional outbursts over something small, and seeing the same patterns playing out in relationships, money and family.

It makes sense now, as my dad was away, my mum was almost like a single parent in those times, having to look after me and my brother, doing all the house things and school runs and cooking and everything else, which meant less time present with us. Less connection and feelings of safety.

Whenever I hurt myself it was a case of 'You'll be OK, it's not that bad.' I'm guilty of this myself as a parent, as I'm sure many of you are, too. This isn't me telling you you're doing everything wrong: it's an education, to stop repeating the past generations' way of parenting. An understanding that at our core we want to feel safe; taking a moment to really see your child in that moment and hold them, letting them know they are safe and loved, allowing them to complete that stress loop leading to self-regulation and training their nervous system to be able to do that naturally when they are older.

I wish I'd known then what I know now, but it's never too late to change. Remember, you're human. With new understanding, old wounds can be healed – for both you and your children. Together, we can break the cycle.

PRECONSCIOUS/PRECOGNITIVE TRAUMA

This is connected to the period of life before the age of eighteen and twenty-four months old, including in the womb. Between eighteen and twenty-four months old a part of the brain comes 'online' and from that point onwards you can start to recall events that happen to you. Before this time that part of the brain is not online. However, as I've been saying, it's not just the mind that remembers things but the body remembers too; the felt sense. In the healing world you hear the word 'soma' or 'somatic': connecting to your body and the emotions being held in it.

There are studies showing women who have prenatal stress have babies with higher levels of cortisol. The baby's nervous system communicates with the mother's and adapts based on the signals they receive from their mum before they are born so they are prepared for the stressed environment they are going into. Such babies are often restless, clingy, attached.[13]

Similarly, if the connection isn't there when the baby is born then the nervous system adapts to that and feels alone, a sense of *I don't belong here* or developing the sense over their first three years that *I'm not safe, I'm unlovable, I'm not good enough*.

Learning about this type of trauma hurt as I know this is the experience of my daughter. I was in a very bad flare-up when I was pregnant. I was in a constant heightened state of stress and over the years I've heard her say 'No one loves me, I can't do anything right, you don't want me here.' Now I have the knowledge about where this comes from, I work on helping her to feel safe and loved and let her know it's OK to feel angry and frustrated, but before I knew this, I used to lose my shit on a regular basis with her and we'd have horrendous screaming matches. All I was doing then was re-enforcing her nervous systems response, embedding them deeper into her body and deepening her beliefs that it's not safe here and she is unloved. Fuck, that was a painful realisation I can tell you.

Even armed with the information regarding my daughter's preconscious trauma, I still fuck up and shout back or lose my shit. In (or after) those moments, I have to remind myself that I'm not perfect, that I'm only human and I still have things I have to work on myself (not that it stops me in the moment from crying and telling myself I'm a shit mum and I'm fucking everything up).

INTERGENERATIONAL TRAUMA

This is where trauma can become intergenerational. Remember how our nervous system adapts to help us survive threats, and if we don't process the experience fully, it becomes imprinted in our nervous system as trauma? Well, that imprint can be passed down to the next generation. As I mentioned earlier with preconscious trauma, there's communication between the baby's and mother's nervous systems. The adaptations your mother's nervous system has made throughout her lifetime can continue to influence yours, carrying on the legacy of unresolved trauma. There is increasingly strong evidence that M.E./CFS is heritable.[14]

It was thought for a long time that you are just your genes, however, there is a field of biology called 'epigenetics' which studies how your behaviours and environment can cause changes that affect the way your genes work. Epigenetic changes are reversible and do not change your DNA sequence but they can change how your body reads a DNA sequence. Your environment and behaviours, such as diet and exercise, can result in epigenetic changes.[15] Think of it like turning a gene on or off based on what you put into your body and what or who your surround yourself with.

It is because of this you may find yourself having the same reaction as your parents. I spoke to my mum about this and we could see it in a few different things. The one that stood out was the fact that I have always had awful anxiety at the thought of having to ring someone, to the point it could set off my symptoms due to the stress running through my body switching me instantly into a survival response. Because my mum experienced the exact same thing, she recognised it in me when I was younger and she would make phone calls for me because she understood the terror I felt.

There was a study done on mice in which male mice received a shock on their feet and at the same time the scent of cherry blossom was sprayed into the cage. The shock they felt would induce a traumatic response and they'd run to the corner of the cage in an anxious state. After repeating this a few times they no longer needed to be shocked; just spraying them with the cherry blossom scent would activate the traumatic response and they'd run to the corner of the cage in an anxious state. These mice then reproduced, but their offspring were never shocked on their feet, so never had the initial trauma. However, if a cherry blossom scent was sprayed into the cage, they would have an anxious traumatic response and run to the corner of the cage. That response then happened to their own babies. That's two generations of traumatic imprinting being passed down.[16]

COLLECTIVE TRAUMA

This is like the big-scale trauma that hits a whole community or even the entire world. Think Covid-19! We all had to adjust to survive, but now those changes are causing a lot of ongoing pain. There is now a diagnosis for those who never seemed to fully recover from Covid-19 called Long Covid, which is very similar to M.E./CFS. Personally, it just feels like another label that fits a bit better into society than M.E./CFS. During Covid-19, the stress loop never completed, they never found that connection of safety again, therefore it continues to live in the body as trauma.

Babies born during the Covid-19 pandemic tuned their nervous systems to match their mums' stress levels, which might've made them more used to high-stress situations. Plus, these little ones missed out on early contact that stimulates their ventral vagus nerve, crucial for feeling connected and secure. On the flip side, babies born before Covid-19 adapted to their world through early developmental responses, sometimes feeling like the world's not a safe place right from the start – some even carry this stress from before they were born. So, babies born during Covid-19 not only deal with their own stuff but also inherit some of the collective stress from the pandemic.

CHAPTER 15

Trauma And Understanding Triggers

Now that you understand the mental and physical impact of unprocessed life experiences, it's time to grasp what triggers these responses. Imagine unprocessed experiences (trauma) as trapped memories where stored information is based on your senses (because everything is initially stored as sensory input). It's this stored information that gets triggered.

Similarly, if you think of a file or a picture stored on your computer, you can click to request more information about the picture such as the type of file it is, where it is stored, when it was created, the size of it. Your memories work in the exact same way. Each memory holds information about that memory, like the emotion or emotions you experienced in that moment, the beliefs you hold around it and so much more.

Its response to the trauma is always there inside your mind and body, alive in your system and it can be triggered or reignited at any moment by something that vaguely represents the original event or circumstances. This can be things you see, hear, smell, taste, feel or a specific emotion or person attached to that original event. Once triggered, that data file opens and out comes all your coping mechanisms and reactions that you needed to survive during the original event. This will then affect how you respond, what action you take and how you behave in the present triggering moment.

A memory of my own

I stood frozen in place as he shouted, a bellowing that set my insides vibrating. The sheer fear rising, I feel so sick, my legs are so tense. Oh god, I think I might pee myself. Keep the eye contact, keep the eye contact. Aargh, I want to look away, to cry, to not be here. I have to keep eye contact as I can't bear to hear the order 'Look at me when I am talking to you.' The anger and disappointment that's coated in those words are like a dagger to the heart. I'm useless, I'm not good enough, I'm bad, I'm wrong. He's so angry, his face is reddening, he seems so tall, my neck hurts looking up, he seems like a giant or maybe I'm shrinking. I can't move, I can't breathe, why do I feel so small, so insignificant? I apologise quietly, my eyes welling up and immediately finding the floor for safety. I still can't move, my feet still stuck to the floor. Does he want me to stay where I am or to get out of his sight? It's safer to wait just in case I make a mistake and the sickening bellowing begins again.

Thirteen years later, she tightens her fist, her face reddens, she begins screaming and shouting. It's so loud I freeze in place, taken right back to being that little girl, petrified to move. I remember I'm not that little girl, I am the mother of the screaming girl. I shout back now; I have a voice now. I let rip, the neighbours can probably hear me, I don't care, I'm so angry, I'm so mad. Why doesn't she listen to me? What did I do wrong?

Shit. I am repeating the cycle. This is not OK, I must do better, I don't want her to feel all that fear I felt.

This isn't what I envisioned for myself and my daughter. Yet, it's been a recurring pattern for years because we absorb what we're exposed to – it becomes ingrained in our nervous system, operating on autopilot. Just as it did for my parents and their parents before them, as I discussed in the previous chapter on intergenerational trauma. It's only when you become aware of your behaviours, actions, and triggers that you can actively choose a different path. Once I learnt about traumas and triggers, I learnt that it doesn't have to be this way. I can put the work in and build a better relationship with my children. I can't undo the traumas I've already caused them but I can choose to be better. It's never too late to hold your hands up and say *I fucked up!*

Triggers allow you to feel a wound that hasn't been fully released from the body. You will feel something in your physical body when someone says or does something and you will instantly want to 'clap' back at them, like a knee-jerk reaction. It happens before you have time to think. It is an unconscious response; it is not something you actively decide in that moment.

A triggered response could be anything from fear, panic, flashbacks, freezing, shutting down, experiencing intense emotional pain, and so forth, along with any physical symptoms associated with these emotions (shaking, loss of appetite, dissociation, fatigue etc.).

You can be triggered by people, situations, events and even social media. When you've become aware of your trigger don't tiptoe around it: it's time to dive deep to claim back your power and integrate that part of yourself back into wholeness. You are retrieving a part of yourself each time you do this work, nurturing and soothing yourself, becoming more and more whole with each step that you take. Digging this deep and uncovering what's there will feel hard at times, but it's so worth it and you can do it.

The person or situation that triggers you is not the problem or issue, they are just the flame and you are the match. My daughter's scream was triggering me, a scream that vibrated through my body. That was the triggering moment. Everything after that was nothing to do with her, it was an expression of hurt and anger, a fear of unworthiness that was unresolved and therefore imprinted and rerunning for all these years.

My response was everything I wanted to do as my younger self in those moments with my dad. My daughter was everything I was too scared to be: to stand my ground, to have a voice, the very expression that I was shut down for having as a child.

Did I want to be this screaming mum? No! How could I change it? I first had to recognise what was happening: that I was being triggered. Then I had to pause, to take a breath and walk away if I needed to. Reminding myself that I'm not that little girl frozen in time waiting for permission. This allowed me space until I was ready to come back to my daughter and talk through the issue she was actually having herself. Letting her know it's OK to feel angry and want to scream but there also needs to be a balance of expression that lies beneath the anger. This is still an ongoing process for me and my daughter. Though our screaming matches are very rare, I still fuck up and lose my shit, just nowhere near the scale I used to. There are also plenty of days when I feel proud, knowing I've been able to hold space for her to feel and know I love her even when she screams at me.

I recognise that she will likely hold her own traumas from the years of shouting at each other, where she didn't feel loved, heard or seen as my ego made everything about me. All I can do now is hold myself in compassion and remind myself I did the best I could with the resources I had at the time. And if she comes to me in a few years with anything about her childhood, I will hear her, I will understand that pain and help her in any way I can. It will be hard, so hard, and it will hurt like hell but I cannot tell her she is wrong when that is what her experiences were to her and that is how they have been stored within her mind and body.

Learning all this took time and patience: the key was building my self-awareness, learning to become an observer of the responses and behaviours I had. I didn't always notice them in the moment or even just after; sometimes it took hours or days before I realised I'd been triggered. So if you are learning this process yourself, please be kind to yourself. It takes time and patience but it does get easier.

You know you are triggered when you were in a specific emotional and physical state, e.g. in a good mood, calm, happy and then that emotional or physical state instantly changes to something else, e.g. rage, fury, anger. When you notice these things happening you can look at them, taking a closer look at the root cause.

You could even assume you have a big trauma when in actual fact it stems from a small trauma. It was only last year that I discovered this for myself. I have always had driving anxiety, specifically when I'm on my own. After getting a good grip on my general anxiety I thought I was good with driving, until I had to take my son to his football game. Then it all came flooding back.

Mum rang, she can't come with me today. Shit, I'm going to have to do this on my own. No problem, I'm great at doing things now.

Wonderful, I drove here easily, feeling a little shaky but that's OK, I'm here now.

My god that's a lot of teams. So many people. Find other parents, you will be fine. Shit, my legs are not feeling good. Fuck, I think I'm getting tremors. Fuck, fuck, fuck. Not now, not with all these people around.

Find somewhere to sit. There, a dry spot by the building. OK, I'm safe. Right?! Why do I feel like I can't breathe? Shit, focus on your breath, Katie, you are fine. You've done this a hundred times. My hands are shaking, my body hurts to fight back the tremors. Oh fuck, now I'm going to cry. I can't cry here. Keep it together, just breathe.

I have to get up to watch him play. You've got this, just stand and do what you have to. Game's over, quick, go sit back down.

Matthew's coming over, quick smile, hold the tears back. He asks if I'm OK. I tell him my legs aren't feeling too great. He's off with his friends again.

He's playing again, quick get up. Shit, the tears keep coming. Quick, wipe them away so no one sees. Matthew comes off the pitch: he knows, I know he knows. He says I can go back to the car. My heart. I'm going to sob hysterically any minute. Keep it together a little longer.

I've not even left the field before the tears really start streaming. Isabelle's in the car. She looks confused. I tell her the anxiety was just too much today but I'll be OK. She hands me tissues as I sit sobbing in the car. I can't stop crying, Isabelle passed me so many tissues I lost count. I apologised for not being able to stop, she said, 'It's OK, you just need to let it out.' My heart again.

I was so annoyed when I got home. Why was this happening? I remembered everything I'd learnt and put it into practice. I asked my mind to show me the image I keep from when I first experienced anxiety for driving on my own (there is always an image attached). A quick flash of a memory came up. It was me and my mum standing in the doorway of the front room, I asked what time we would be leaving tomorrow for my race. Her reply, 'I'm not taking you, you can drive now, take yourself.' Her hand flicking as if brushing me away and her voice sounded so sharp, like I was being an inconvenience.

Boom, there it was: the moment when the driving anxiety took root. To begin processing this new information I began asking myself questions.

1. What was it about that moment that caused a wound in me?

    I felt like she didn't care, like she was done with me. I felt rejected, abandoned even. Ooh, powerful.

2. Is it true? Did your mum reject or abandon you?

    No, not once. Quite the opposite in fact. She has been by my side every day caring for me.

3. Is there anything else that you notice or have become aware of about this stored memory?

    Yes, as I think about it, Mum would never have spoken to me that way. I think I stored it that way because it felt absurd and out of nowhere. When really she probably said in just her normal mum tone, like any other conversation. And even though my memory shows her hand brushing me away, I think that too is a lie. It's just not like her to do that, it was just what I felt she was doing to me figuratively.

4. Now you know this is a lie and just a reaction to a fifteen-second encounter, can you let this go today?

    Yes, it was not true. It is a false memory and therefore a false reaction and a false belief.

ANXIETY EXERCISE – THANK YOUR FUTURE SELF

When you find yourself becoming anxious about something, this technique can help:

1. Notice that you're experiencing anxiety
2. Identify what you are feeling anxious about
3. Recall a similar situation where you felt anxious. If you can't recall something similar, focus on any past experience of anxiety
4. Ask yourself, *But did I die though?* This can help to lighten the intensity and bring the level of drama down to a more manageable level. Acknowledge that you didn't die – otherwise, you wouldn't be reading this book – and recognise that you survived the situation
5. Recall other times when you lived through similar anxiety
6. Remind yourself that you successfully faced and overcame those situations. Recognise your own resilience and ability to navigate through challenges each time
7. Visualise your future self handling the situation with ease and grace. Connect with the feeling of confidence that you will survive the event
8. Now, affirm to yourself, *I thank my future self for knowing exactly what to do in the moment, as they always do. I no longer need to carry this burden.*

9. Repeat the above affirmation as often as necessary while envisioning your future self being strong, capable, and fucking awesome. You've got this!

EXERCISE TO USE WHEN YOU NOTICE YOURSELF BEING TRIGGERED

I use this exercise often when I reflect on a moment, interaction or event where I reflect and think, *What the fuck just happened?*

1. Become aware of when you are being triggered. The first step is to recognise that you've even been triggered. It's likely you will have that 'knee-jerk' reaction, possibly say something nasty or hurtful, or blame whatever or whoever it was that triggered you, like wanting to bring them down. You will throw straight back at the person, situation or event without a second's thought; an automatic response.
2. Ask yourself, *Did I feel like this two seconds ago?*
3. Then ask, *What was it that triggered me specifically?* Was it the tone, the person, the body language, the word, the phrase?
4. Clearly identify the thoughts, feelings or actions associated with the situation making you uncomfortable. It can present itself as anger, rage, blame, name-calling, putting someone else down or thinking it's not your fault. Use the wheel of emotions at the end of this chapter to help if you struggle to identify your emotions. You may feel more than one emotion.
5. Ask yourself, *Am I throwing this back on someone?*
6. Take the focus off the external situation and focus within yourself.
   Check in and ask, *What is arising?*

7. Give it a name: anxiety, craving, insecurity etc. Write it down.
8. *Remember*: it is *never* the other person, so separate yourself from the immediate situation triggering you.
9. Now take a step back and look at it objectively with no judgement. Reflect on the trigger that you've become aware of. You may find memories pop up as you take some time to reflect.
10. Ask yourself, *What is being revealed? What deeper belief is appearing?* For example, *I'm worthless. I'm not good enough. I'm ugly. I'm not lovable. I'm pathetic. I will always lose. I always get hurt.*
11. Question the following, *Can I identify patterns from this thought, feeling, or action? Is there a belief I hold about myself? Does it get triggered often?*

Triggers are layered so as you become aware of one thing you will find other thoughts, feelings, or memories may appear. Lean into the discomfort, try not to avoid anything.

When you are met with resistance allow yourself space and breathe allowing stuck energy to move through you. Any resistance that crops up will highlight patterns, so become aware of what you may suddenly want to do instead of dealing with the discomfort: avoidance, denial, numbing and dissociating are all common traits of resistance.

There is no blame or judgement when working on yourself, only awareness and compassion.

12. Now you have found your trigger, identified it, recognised its patterns, programming and the limiting belief behind it, you can now transcend it.

    Ask yourself, *Do I want to continue with this programming or rewrite it?*

    It's time to write a new narrative that is in alignment with your true self.

    Remember, you *always* get to choose again!

    Example – Anxiety stems from fear and has you believing in the worst possible outcome.

    New narrative – *I believe in the best-case scenario. My past does not define me. I am safe and am always being guided by something greater than me. Anything is possible for me and I trust my future self to know what I need in the moment.*

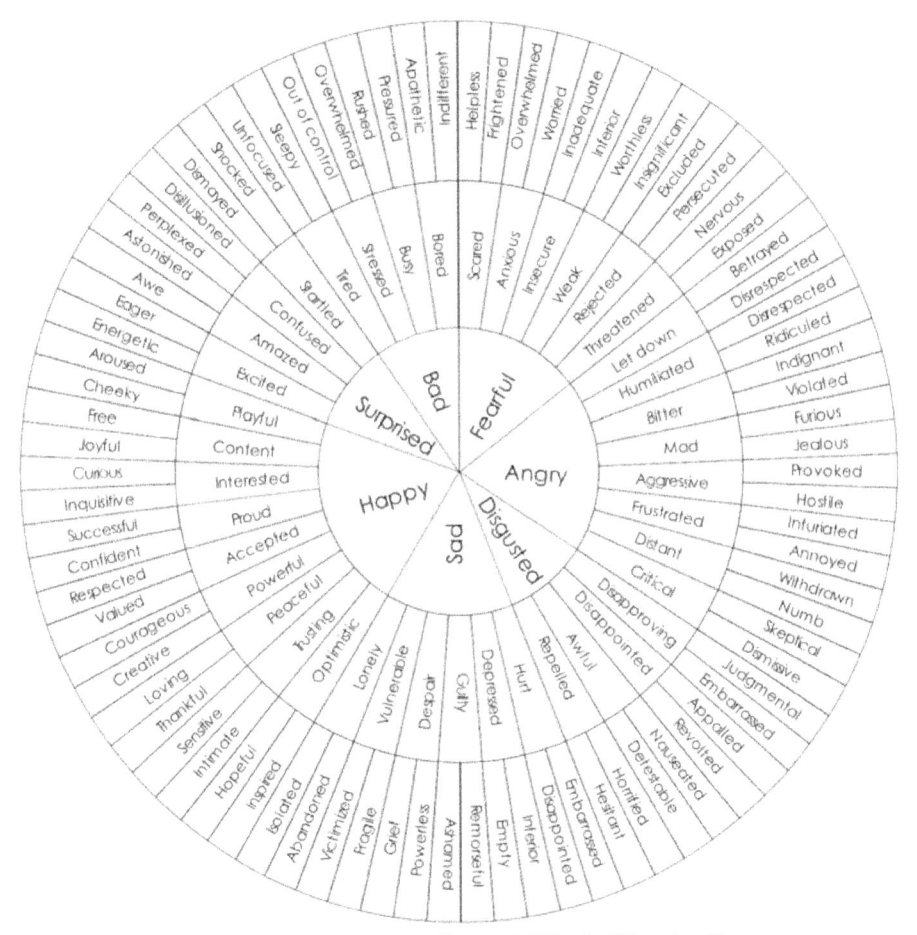

Figure 6. Wheel of Emotions[17]

CHAPTER 16

Uncovering Trauma

The battle you unknowingly began when the trauma occurred becomes an ongoing war inside you. It gets programmed into your mind, your body, your nervous system, organs, cells: your entire being. It becomes a part of your life, a part of who you believe you are. It's your new 'normal'.

This is why it is so important to build your knowledge and awareness as to what trauma is, the impact it can have on you and the effect it can have on your life. Knowing that the inner voice you've listened to for so long is not actually the friend you think it is, and holding its proverbial hand all this time, thinking it would save you from drowning in your sorrow, your pain, your anguish, has led you into self-entrapment.

This is not who you are. You are both the darkness and the light. There is something much better on the other side waiting for you, waiting for you to reclaim the spark to light you up again.

Do not let the deafening roar from within harbour you like a fugitive any longer. Set yourself free. Yes, it takes time, effort and commitment. As the old saying goes, *Rome wasn't built in a day.* You did not get to this place in a day, it was an ebb and flow, a gentle tug here and there until you could no longer tread the water and found yourself pulled under.

That is where you have been trying to survive from: a place that dampens your senses, your true inner voice, your gut instinct, your higher self; whatever you prefer to call it. It's been lingering deep within, waiting to come to the surface, to be heard once more. The voice you've been following is not your truth. It's the layers of protection, of coping strategies to survive the hand you were dealt when you didn't have the resources to overcome the trauma.

The most beautiful thing about your mind is that it knows when to hide things that you are not ready to deal with and it also knows when you are ready to face them. The trickier part is the conscious side of the mind, the ego that says no. It feels scary, uncomfortable, like if we let one thing out it will all come flooding out. The truth is when the mind starts presenting you with the truth, it knows you are ready to handle it, because remember the mind's prime directive is to protect you, no matter what.

How many times have you had a memory or thought that flashed in your mind and you've cringed or felt something deeply uncomfortable? Those are the moments that your true self is communicating to you, letting you know it is safe now, to face this, to resolve the emotion, the feeling, the sensation that it is connected to.

The mind works through symbolism so it tends to show you images, memories, songs, phrases, or you just have this 'knowing' of something, and it can be at the most random parts of your day, like washing your dishes or driving your car. There is no reason for it to appear other than it needing to be addressed. It can be as simple as saying 'Thank you, I am aware of what you're showing me and I am ready to release this from my mind, body and spirit today.' This might sound a bit 'out there' and far too simple – I know, I thought the same. But now I use it time and time again. Awareness is key to your evolution: it is the spirit in you guiding you because the truth is you already know what you need, it is just the ego mind and programming that gets in your way.

There are times when some things need more awareness than you may realise. You often need to really feel whatever has arisen before you can let it go. Maybe you just need a good cry and you don't know why. That's OK, you don't always need to know why. It's about getting out of your own head and dropping into your body; the felt sense or soma. I just call it the body's language because it felt like learning a whole new language when I learnt how to do this. Doing this helps you release stuck, stagnant emotions from your body. I am a big fan of sound healing and what I refer to as 'inner work journeys' for this type of healing (there's more to come on sound healing and other types of healing later in the book).

And yes, there are the tougher, more stubborn unprocessed experiences that need questioning. A sprinkling of curiosity. You can do this yourself with the tools I've shared in the past few chapters, as well as those in the upcoming chapters, or you may need to seek professional help to guide you through the heavier stuff.

I did a vast majority of facing my shit on my own, in many different formats, which I will continue to share with you throughout the book. Indeed, I say 'on my own' but I believe spiritually I was supported along the way. My intuition guiding me more and more with each step I took back to wholeness.

When I got stuck – because I did get stuck a lot of times throughout the years – I found myself constantly avoiding things I knew deep down I should have been addressing. I would avoid it for a few months sometimes. Why? Because I was protecting myself from what my unconscious already knew: it was going to be painful, it wasn't going to be fun to face what was coming up, so avoiding was one of my ways to cope. This is when I should have sought outside help. Someone to guide me through the resistance. I eventually learnt to ask for help and also to use the tools and techniques I had to finally address what was coming up, because the more you avoid it, the more it keeps trying to come up until eventually you'll be forced to just face it. I'm stubborn like that.

Recently (May 2023) I had this exact thing happen. I knew there was something I had to confront about my marriage. I didn't want to. It was too big. It was years of unspoken things, behaviours and words that were just the 'norm' now. I'd peeled a small bit back and what I revealed to myself was that I felt like I owed Lee. He had stuck around all these years. *How dare I question his behaviours, his words, his actions after everything he had to live with. I owe him. I would be a horrible human being if I demanded more. He's already given so much.*

Ignoring these feelings and pushing them down led to this moment...

Run ... hide ... that uncovering was too much, it hurt my heart too much. There's so much more bubbling under the surface. I don't like what it might mean if I look deeper. Protect, protect, protect. Months have gone by; I had a cold, another month went, I got a worse cold. I play football with my son and I literally face-plant the concrete, leaving two scars on my face and a constantly bruised-looking knee. The

153

years have taught me all these things have meaning, especially the physical body. I looked up the meaning of the face and knee (face represents what we show the world, knee represents pride and ego), but I still can't face it; it feels overwhelming and so scary.

Avoid, avoid, avoid. Darkness is starting to creep in, my body is so heavy, fatigue is creeping in more and more as the days go by. I'm crying most days. I need to escape; I want to run away. I can't stay here, I can't be a mum, I can't be a wife. I'm not what they need. Books, fantasies, I need to escape, I need a different world to live in. I devour book after book. I've now read 14 books in one month, averaging 550 pages each, most books done in less than 2 days. I barely read 4 books last year. Every time I close the book the chaos of my mind hits me like a wave, chaos swirling again. I'm back in my reality. I don't like it here, it's too much, it's too painful. I open another book, the voices quieten, I relax, I can breathe, I'm safe.

I'm lying in the bath, I can barely move, there's a constant fog in my mind and my thoughts scare me. I curl into the foetal position, wedged against the sides. I'm crying again; not sobbing, just a constant stream of tears rolling down. I want to escape. I hear a shadow of a voice, Just unwedge your foot from the side of the bath, you could let the water take you, you could have silence, you could be free from all this noise.

Lee comes in, sees me curled up, he asks what's wrong. I try to find my words. I just cry more as I finally tell him everything is too much. He asks what is? Between the uncontrollable weeping I manage to squeal out, 'I don't want to be here any more.' *He doesn't know what to do in this situation. He never has, it's why I've never said it out loud to him before. He tries his best, I see his body tense, trying to find words, searching his mind for what to do or say. Words he doesn't have. I feel rejected, abandoned. The voice is right, it would be better if I wasn't here. Fear ... so much fear starts to flood my body.*

Katie, move, get out, NOW! *I hear a different voice in my head. It takes everything I have left to drag myself out of the bath.*

Next bath, it happens again, this time the voice is louder, so much louder. I ask Lee to stay with me. I'm scared of what I may do if I'm on my own. I say it all out loud, I tell Lee all the thoughts, I tell him everything my mind is telling me. How crippling it is. I need him to know. I need to speak it out loud. Then I won't be on my own. He's listening. He's trying to be there for me in his own way. I get out the bath, I Google mental health facilities. This isn't how I go out. I've faced far worse, overcome so much, even this very same voice. I can beat this.

I was ready: I had to face what I had been ignoring. I used what I knew to begin the process. One day I thought *I'm physically better now, I could actually go for a run.* I knew there was evidence of exercise helping with improving symptoms of depression so I figured I had nothing to lose in trying. I didn't expect to be back running, but it was working. Instead of checking into a mental health facility for myself, because honestly, I couldn't find any information to be able to check myself in. Instead, I booked a four-day break, just for me. No bath, just a shower. I finally rang Salli, who had been checking in on me because I'd been so quiet but I couldn't face talking to her before. Three hours of sobbing down the phone and it felt good to finally say it all out loud: my marriage was not in a good place, I'd become overwhelmed by doing everything and being everything to everyone. It wasn't sustainable. Real conversations finally happened. What I would and wouldn't accept. What I wanted, like being hugged or knowing what Lee really thought, not what he thought I wanted to hear. I needed truth, authenticity and I needed help around the house. I wanted my marriage to work but I wasn't willing to have a mental breakdown for it, not any more.

It is not a weakness to ask for help: it is growth, it is progression, movement, it takes you forward. It is bravery and strength. I could have avoided all of that if I had just faced things when they first came up. I wouldn't change it though. Things have been changing at home. A new appreciation and respect have emerged not just from Lee but the kids too. I had lessons I had to learn, things I had to realise and I wouldn't be back running if it wasn't for that lapse in sanity. All this was possible because of the work I'd previously put in, like going to counselling, having coaching, using tools and techniques that I found work for me. My most effective ones are those I share with you in the following chapters.

CHAPTER 17

The Ups And Downs Of Living With M.E.

Let's now come back to my experience of M.E./CFS and my tumultuous journey to heal. So far, I've described my encounters with various 'specialists' from my diagnosis in 2008 until the catastrophic appointment with the neurologist around between 2014 or 2015.

We need to go back to 2015 (after the counselling sessions, neurologist, psychologist and all the other '–ologists' sessions). When I applied to go back to university to study sports and nutrition. At this same time, we had put an offer in to buy our own house, a doer-upper. We were living in the house I described in chapter 9, with the downstairs bathroom. My symptoms had become 'stable', meaning I wasn't in the wheelchair as much, and I mostly used my crutches (aka Clive) to get around, especially outside. Things seemed quite good: we were finally going to own our own house and I was going to make something of myself.

Then there was a day I will never forget because of the intensity of the emotions I felt.

I had friends I'd see every few months and they came over for a catch up. There was nothing different in the way we shared, laughed and caught everyone up on all things life. I was feeling so happy and excited for each of them as they shared all their exciting updates, all of which I knew they'd worked so hard for and had wanted for so long.

As we sat there in my conservatory and they continued chatting, I suddenly became very aware of how I was constantly trying to stop the tremors brewing under my skin and I found myself trying so hard to hide the pain I was in, making jokes to deflect as a twitch or spasm would break free. Never really answering the 'How are you doing?' I couldn't, I didn't know how to tell them that most days I was completely broken, that I was so exhausted to the point I didn't know how to stay here, that I just wanted a hug, I just wanted someone to sit with me, to rock me and tell me everything was going to be OK. My whole body was in such a state of tension, it was a battle to even sit there. I couldn't because I knew deep down that if I did, I would break and if I broke, I'd never stop crying. Plus, at that time I believed there wasn't anything that anyone could do for me.

Instead, I told them how great I was doing, that I was going back to university. I know now that I only decided to go back to university because I thought I would become someone, I'd have a new identity, I'd be more than this illness. I just hadn't realised that all that 'brokenness', the pain and despair hadn't gone away even though I was 'stable'. Deep down every day really was a fight to stay here.

I had yet again tricked myself into thinking I was doing better. I wasn't doing better. Every day, I still needed help to get around, I couldn't leave the house on my own, anxiety and depression were just always there, a constant hum of my life and the tremors were like a ticking time bomb that lived inside me, never knowing when it might go off. It was like I was being held captive and being tortured by my own body.

When my friends left that day, I thanked them for coming, I smiled so brightly and it was true, I was grateful they'd come to see me; they were the only people I saw outside of my family but what hit me after they left was beyond overwhelming. As the last car left, I fell to the floor like someone had flicked a switch and I was overcome with so many emotions, too many to name. I cried, no, I wailed, I screamed with so much pain, so much anger, so much sadness, grief and loss. It was raw emotional pain: everything I had forced myself to keep in when they were there and everything I had locked away as I told myself I was doing better hit me like a tidal wave. I felt like I was drowning and I didn't know which way was up.

I was angry that their lives were moving on. Angry that they couldn't see that I needed help, or maybe they did but didn't know how to help me and, let's be honest, I wouldn't have accepted the help anyway, I would have pushed it away and made a joke about it all. I was angry at myself for telling myself that they didn't really want to know the truth of how dark it had got in my head, that I would just become a burden to them too if I told them, that there wasn't anything they could do for me in any case.

After this I found myself falling into a deep depression (the one I mentioned in chapter 11) and we moved back in with Mum. My symptoms got even worse and I reverted to hardly being able to function at all, I became a zombie, I was just a shell of a person. I'd become so numb. I ended up not starting university and we also pulled out of buying the house because of how much needed doing: it was too much work and pressure to put on Lee when I was in such a state. I couldn't get out of bed on my own; Lee had to carry me or at least help me downstairs to the sofa (I refused to stay in bed, I knew if I stayed there, I'd fall deeper into the darkness. I *had* to get up and I *had* to get changed. To feel somewhat human).

We moved back to my mum's at the end of 2015 when everything had just become too much, not just for me but for Lee too. I can't even imagine what he was going through and thinking at the time. He doesn't speak about it and when I have asked in the past he just shrugs and says 'I just got on with it.' This was now the third or fourth time we'd moved back in with Mum. I don't know how my mum managed to put up with us so many times, but she was always there, without fail.

At Mum's, I became mostly bedridden; I couldn't live in the same way as I did in the old house because the bathroom was upstairs at Mum's and the tremors were always lingering right under the surface … my body had become completely unpredictable. There were still some good days – or what seemed like good days. It's funny because a 'good day' to a normal person is not the same as a 'good day' to someone with a chronic illness. When I was having a good day, it meant the fatigue and pain was manageable, the anxiety wasn't preventing me from leaving the house. If I switched bodies with a normal person, they'd think something was terribly wrong but that is the reality of a chronic illness. It all becomes so normal to us that we adjust our expectations, we can't even remember what it feels like to feel normal. This is the nervous system adapting so you can survive, as I mentioned in chapter 12.

Those good days, however, could easily turn into nightmare days. Not always, but I never knew which good days would last for the full day and which ones wouldn't. When we first moved in with Mum, I'd wake up feeling good, able to get around the house, and everyone would leave for work and school thinking I'd be fine for the day.

One day, I was in the kitchen getting a snack and making a cuppa, walking round pretty well. As I began to walk from one side of the kitchen to the other for my cup of tea, I suddenly found my face just inches away from the cold, hard tiled floor. A rush of anger raced through me as I screamed in frustration, 'You fucking stupid body, why now? Where the fuck did that come from? How the hell am I going to get back upstairs?'

I managed to crawl to my crutches but it was pointless, my legs barely held me and my body was spasming and twitching so badly it looked like I was possessed. I lay on the cold floor running various scenarios through my head: I couldn't stay on the floor all day. I crawled around the kitchen, still experiencing tremors and spasms, I found a tray to fill up with food for lunch, snacks, drinks and a cuppa. As I was rummaging around, I found my selfie stick so I decided to film the process of getting back upstairs. I don't know why I decided to do this, maybe it was to distract myself, but I ended up sharing it on social media to show what a chronic illness could look like on my worst days, the days when people don't see me. You can find this video on my website and a clip of that day is included in it if you fancy a nosey. You can find it at www.hope-light.co.uk/about.

I began crawling through the kitchen, across the longest front room known to mankind, to reach the base of the stairs. I had to stop so many times along the way, needing a longer pause before I could tackle the mammoth task of climbing Mount Everest: the stairs. I took one step at a time; I was already exhausted. I held on to the wooden spindles of the banister, crying as my whole body was shaking while I used all the strength in my arms to lift my body weight up each step, all while carefully manoeuvring the tray alongside me. I finally made it to the top of the stairs, only to be faced with the fucking corridor. Of course my bedroom was at the end of the house! (It was that one because it was next to the bathroom).

On days like this I just wanted to curl up and die. I was done, it was exhausting being me, being on my own, having only my voice to listen to. One part screaming, anger bursting out of the seams of my mind, the other encouraging, telling me I can do this. I made it back to my bed and I broke. I cried and my body spasmed out. I didn't know how to exist in these moments, when it felt like it was never going to end. It was pure torture.

From that day on we made sure I had some food and drink next to the bed but there were still days we couldn't prepare for. There really is no describing the screams, the anger, the tantrums I experienced in those months at Mum's. Those *WHY?!* And *I FUCKING HATE YOU!* moments. Like someone had done this to me.

There was another day when my legs failed me before I made it back to bed and I had so little energy I couldn't lift myself to climb up to the bed. I lay on the floor crying for a long time, until I eventually decided I had to do something. I did what I never do: I rang a friend who lived down the road and she came straight up to help. I just needed to be put in the bed but she refused to leave me and said she'd take me to her house as one of her kids was home poorly. After some hilarious antics to get me down the stairs and out to the car, she took me to her house for the day where I watched kids' films with her little one and had food and drinks made for me, so pretty much a win-win all round.

That was the first time I had ever allowed anyone to see me in that way, outside of my family. There was something that always made me feel like a burden, or like I was weak if I showed someone how broken I was. There was a shame I felt. I remember being so frustrated. I was living on a constant rollercoaster and I was just so angry and frustrated that every time I felt like I was getting some kind of balance I would always end up paying for it. At this point in my life I was just so fed up: I'd seen a neurologist, psychiatrist and psychologist and still had no answers, no direction in where to look for help; it all just felt so hopeless. I became a shell of a person, the smiles and laughter were so hard to coax up to the surface. I just felt so numb and alone.

CHAPTER 18

A Shift In Mindset

How is a book going to help me?

So, we've reached the end of 2015 and I'm living with my mum and working in the network marketing business (where I met Salli aka 'the wifey'). When I say 'working,' I mean I was lying in bed, sharing my journey online. It was a job I could do even when my body didn't cooperate, but my mind craved something more meaningful. In this business we were encouraged to read self-development books, which was weird to me. At this point in my life, I hardly ever read books for pleasure let alone these self-development or self-help books, which I'd never heard of before. At first, I thought, *As if a book could help someone.*

    I read the first book while I was mostly bedridden at my mum's house. It was called *Girl Code: Unlocking the Secrets to Success, Sanity, and Happiness for the Female Entrepreneur*. I figured what the hell, I literally have nothing else to do. I could only focus on surviving each day and we needed help with the kids, who were about six and four at the time. I was hardly able to be around them for much more than an hour most days due to extreme fatigue and pain, though mostly it was the sensory overload. Those times when I could barely leave that bed left me feeling like the shittiest mum ever. I honestly feel like I disappeared from their lives entirely at this time. When I try to recall anything from this period it is just a mass of haze. I know I was around them: like I said I have pictures, and I even know there were good days, but I remember so little.

The things I do recall are so silly as well. For instance, I remember getting Steady Eddie (my mobility scooter); I remember redecorating the room so I could have a TV in there so I had everything I needed upstairs (where the bathroom was); I remember a lot of crawling, a lot of tears and a lot of frustration. And I remember reading *Girl Code*.

I read this book just after the severe depression I'd encountered a few months after my counselling sessions (described in chapter 11). I can still recall reading *Girl Code* and feeling something shift inside me: a spark, like hope … that light growing a little bit more. I felt like there was more out there for me, that I can make the best of this shitty situation. I didn't suddenly feel like I could be cured but I did feel like I could live with what I had. I was no longer the prisoner I previously thought myself to be. There was an acceptance.

My mind felt like a door was being blasted open with this golden light spilling out from it. I began to see myself and my life in a different way. I had always thought I was a positive person; people had told me again and again after all, so it must be true. I realised, however, that too was a lie, yet another mask. Two completely different stories were being narrated: the one I was saying to myself out loud (yes, I talk out loud to myself) and the one only I could hear; my internal dialogue. My positive words and outward behaviour were far from what was happening inside my head. Internally, it was a constant battle between not feeling good enough and telling myself, *I've got this!*

This book had suggestions and activities to do so I did them. I began finding the positives in every day. Such things like: I'd made it out of bed, I'd spent more than an hour with the kids, I'd sat outside, I'd made a cuppa, I brushed my teeth standing up, or I'd washed my hair. Once I started doing this daily, I began to look for more simple things I could do for myself and I built it up slowly. There were days when my mind and body fought back but I just kept finding those little things when I could, as often as I could.

There is evidence that reading problem-focused self-help materials can be effective in the treatment of disorders, and even have outcomes comparable to therapist administered treatments.[18] Becoming proactive and seeking help for clinically significant emotional disorders is more effective than being on waiting lists or no treatment conditions.[19]

Although physically I was going through one of the worst periods ever in my life, reading this book had sparked something in me mentally and emotionally. Perhaps that's why I started sharing what I was actually going through with my family. There was an inner strength that allowed me to start overcoming any shame I felt and start asking for help. That's when I made a rare doctor's appointment.

CHAPTER 19

The Doctor Who ACTUALLY Listened

Feeling seen and heard

It was during this time living at my mum's I decided to finally go and see a doctor again. Luckily, this doctor took time to actually listen; he didn't fob me off or make me feel like I was lying.

He explained something to me and it made so much sense, it was the first thing that ever made any sense to me about what I had been experiencing. He told me that sometimes the brain sends the wrong messages to the body, it's like wires get crossed and the outcome is some kind of symptom. In my case it was the tremors. He prescribed me Diazepam, a benzodiazepine as it would help with calming the mind and relaxing the muscles so they weren't so stressed and tense all the time, allowing my brain to remember what it is like to have relaxed muscles.

He even told me about another patient with Psoriasis who had tried all sorts of lotions and potions, until they realised it came from stress on the body and mixed messages being sent to the body. His Psoriasis cleared up after a few weeks. This short conversation made me realise this was exactly what was happening to me. My body was getting the wrong messages all the time. And this was the moment a crack appeared in the door I'd slammed shut after seeing the neurologist, when I'd actively rejected any information about the mind. This doctor, on the other hand, had piqued my curiosity.

This doctor explained it in a way that I could understand. I loved biology and remembered how messages would be sent from the brain to the body to move etc. so I could comprehend what he was explaining to me. Unlike singing a fucking song. In contrast to the neurologist, this doctor took time to make me feel seen. He didn't make me feel like I was making anything up and he explained things with an example of someone else who'd had success. Even though that person didn't have what I had, he explained that it was all coming from the same place: the mind creating messages that were being fired to the rest of my body. I honestly felt like there may be hope for me in that moment.

I was now on Diazepam three times a day, as well as the nutritional supplements I was taking daily anyway. After a week I was feeling like I could relax a bit more and after a few weeks I was walking again; not always perfectly but it was better than I'd been experiencing. It had been so long since I had walked down the stairs. I couldn't believe it. I sat outside when everyone was in work, felt the sun on my face and breathed fresh air into my lungs. I suddenly felt alive again.

That explanation from this doctor got stored in my mind, which would later become something so much bigger.

CHAPTER 20

The Mind

The mind is incredibly complex and there is always more to learn and discover but I thought I'd break down what I know into digestible information. I learnt about the power of the mind about five years after that doctor's appointment. It took time for me to open my mind up to the possibility that there was more to what I was experiencing than just something physical. That there was a deeper mental connection to it as well. I probably would have discovered it a lot sooner if it hadn't been for that neurologist.

I want you to know that what you experience is always real and true but to also know that what you are feeling physically will be connected to the mind, too. They are one, not separate.

When talking about the mind I talk of the conscious and unconscious. There is also the subconscious, but my teachings focus around trauma and trauma is stored in the unconscious part of the mind (as well as the body, obviously), that is what we will be focusing on.

The conscious mind

The conscious mind involves any thoughts and feelings you are currently aware of. What you are feeling, doing, seeing, touching, experiencing. You are conscious of it, or aware of it, like how some memories come easily to the conscious mind as you try to recall something.

The unconscious mind

Your unconscious mind runs the body: it tells your heart when to beat, when to breathe, it adjusts the chemicals in your body, adjusting your hormones. All these things are happening every second without you having to think about it.

Unconscious *thinking* happens deep within the brain and stores the memory of traumatic events that your conscious mind isn't aware of. This is why some people have no recollection of a traumatic event – it has been repressed and buried to protect you. Hypnotherapy is a common practice used to access this deeper part of the mind.

Think of an iceberg: what you see above water is the conscious part and what you don't see is the unconscious part. I also use the iceberg to depict the mind, body, and spirit. The mind being what you see above the water, the body what is below and the water being your spirit: the connection between the mind and body, bringing it together as one.

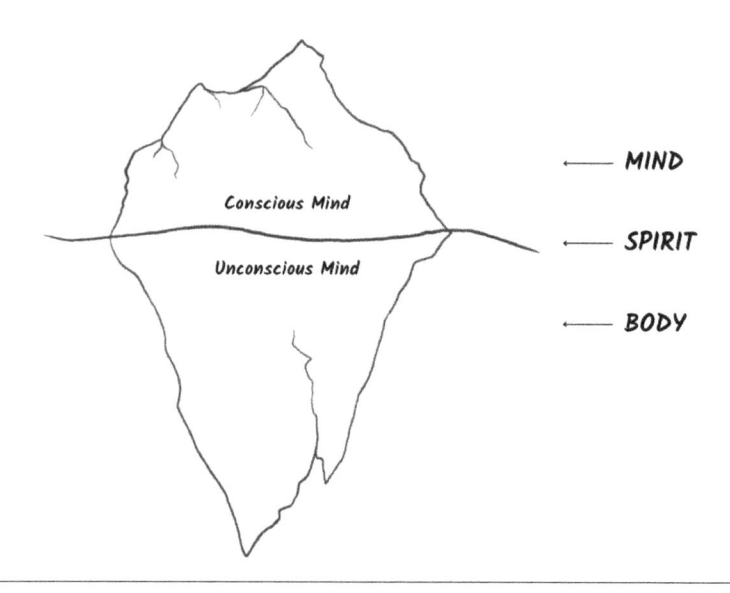

Figure 7: Iceberg of the conscious and unconscious mind

Just because you can't see below the surface doesn't mean it's not there. I think an iceberg is also a very accurate representation of a chronic illness: you can physically see if someone is not OK, such as looking pale, losing weight, looking dead in the eyes like they're not really there, but there is so much more going on at a cellular level inside the body and mind that isn't visible to the naked eye.

You may be able to pretend – or in my case laugh everything off – but you can't escape the pain that spreads through your body like wildfire, the internal screams you choke down as your inner child desperately tries to shout out for help to be saved but that crippling mental chatter tells you, you can't because then you will be judged, shamed or be a burden, so it's safer to keep it all in.

MINDFULNESS

Books will not 'cure' or 'fix' you. So if that is why you're reading this, then I'm sorry to say you'll be disappointed to know that simply reading will not get you your life back. You have to put the work in yourself. Books can, however, open your mind to new possibilities, alternative options and perceptions that you were not taught growing up. I believe there is so much that is missing from the educational system. Children need to learn how to cope with stressful situations, because, let's be honest, we are in a world that asks for more and more from everyone, expecting excellence in return for little reward.

There is a reason why chronic stress is increasing throughout society. According to the Global Organization of Stress, about 450,000 workers in Britain believe their stress is making them ill; 91 per cent of Australians feel stressed about one or more important parts of their life; and in the U.S. psychologists say that if teens between the ninth and twelfth grade don't learn healthy ways to manage that stress now, it could have serious long-term health implications.[20]

If children were taught simple techniques and tools to tackle stress from a young age, as well as being given the knowledge of the mind and body intricacies then they would be better equipped to face the world. When I say simple, I mean simple, like breathing techniques to calm the nervous system and bring their attention back to the present moment. Mindfulness to avoid getting swept away in the *what ifs* of life. We as adults can (and need to!) learn all these things too, remember children are absorbing what is being modelled to them.

Practising mindfulness is extremely beneficial for your mind, body and spirit. It is effective in reducing stress, anxiety and depression, as well as reducing pain and fatigue in people with chronic pain.[21]

There are a variety of different forms of meditation and mindfulness that can be used to help to bring a dysregulated nervous system back into homeostasis, including mindfulness-based stress reduction, Vipassana Meditation, Iyengar Yoga, Transcendental Meditation®, and inward attention meditation.[22]

Mindfulness itself is the practice of being fully present and engaged in the present moment, without judgement or attachment to your thoughts or emotions. It's about paying attention to your thoughts, feelings and bodily sensations in a non-reactive way. You are just watching them, witnessing them, nothing else. Just like clouds in the sky, each thought and feeling has its own unique shape, size and colour. You're not trying to change anything or analyse anything, just observe what is there. The practice is to not become attached but to just say *I see you and that's OK.*

The more you practise the easier it becomes to develop non-judgemental awareness of the present moment. This leads to a greater acceptance of yourself as well as heightening clarity and focus, which all help to reduce stress, improve emotional wellbeing and ignite a sense of empowerment.

What I personally love about mindfulness is that you can practise it anywhere. You don't have to schedule time to sit down and do it. Once you get the hang of what you are doing you can use it throughout your day. Like when you are driving, washing your dishes, eating, walking, even interacting with people.

A body scan is a wonderful practice to build awareness of your physical body and begin to learn the language of your own body. This helps me identify when I am uncomfortable in a situation or if I'm being triggered by someone. It generates the awareness that something has changed in me physically, such as tension in my stomach, holding my breath etc. I have the ability now to stop, breathe and ask myself if I want to participate in this or walk away. Whereas before I would have unconsciously reacted or forced myself to stay because it is what was programmed into me: to be a people-pleaser, and make sure everyone else feels comfortable at the expense of my own health.

If you want to try a body scan meditation, you'll find one on my website; www.hope-light.co.uk/bookresources. Some other great apps are Insight Timer, Headspace, and Calm. And bonus - they're free!

BECOMING THE OBSERVER

Ever notice that constant chatter in your head? Yeah, we all deal with it, especially when stress kicks in or we're just coasting on autopilot. It's easy to get sucked into those thoughts, right?

Becoming the observer is about taking a step back and watching the thoughts roll by, rather than attaching to them. It's all about building your awareness. Without that awareness, you're stuck in the same old rut, blaming everything and everyone except yourself. When you start observing, you catch those unhelpful thoughts in action. And that's when you can choose to respond differently and own your actions. Allowing you to take responsibility and choose to react differently and taking accountability for yourself.

You can't heal what you're not aware of. That's where the practice of presence comes in. But let's be real – it takes time and effort. It's not something that happens overnight. However, if you're sick and resting, you have the time to explore this. Why not give it a try? What have you got to lose?

Throughout this book, you'll find various practices and techniques to help you develop your ability to observe your thoughts and emotions.

GRATITUDE

Gratitude pairs beautifully with mindfulness. When you express gratitude your brain releases dopamine and serotonin, which are two neurotransmitters responsible for your emotions and the feel-good factor. This hormone boost immediately lifts your mood, leaving you feeling happy from the inside out.

The more you practice gratitude, the more dopamine your brain pumps out. Studies suggest that people with low dopamine levels might struggle with memory and slower thinking. So, while dopamine's usually the feel-good hormone, it's also crucial for keeping your brain in good shape.

When you have low levels of dopamine, you're at a higher risk for depression, anxiety, and lack of motivation. Expressing gratitude elevates your dopamine levels, which puts you in a better mood.

While dopamine gives you that feel-good vibe, serotonin is what brings genuine happiness. It not only boosts your mood but also regulates cortisol, improves sleep, and enhances memory and learning – making it a valuable tool for managing conditions like M.E./CFS. When you prioritize gratitude, your mood improves, stress levels decrease, and you'll find yourself better equipped for focus, problem-solving, and decision-making.

By consciously practicing gratitude every day, you can strengthen neural pathways, leading to easier access to a grateful and positive mindset within yourself.

Your mind cannot focus on positive and negative information at the same time, so by practising gratitude, you can train the brain to focus on positive emotions and thoughts. Your day-to-day thoughts don't naturally focus on gratitude. According to a study published by the National Science Foundation, Dr Fred Luskin found that human beings have thousands of thoughts a day (the average person has about 12,000 to 60,000 thoughts per day) and a whopping 80% of them tend to be negative. And get this, 95% of those thoughts are the same old stuff we thought about yesterday!

You can see that one of the tendencies of the mind is to focus on the negative, and it continuously loops these thoughts, which your brain starts to believe. This breeds pessimism and negativity, resulting in limiting beliefs about yourself. This is what was happening to me during 'the cause' I described in chapter 2. If you can break this cycle of negative thinking, then you enable positivity and opportunities to enter your life. All from sprinkling your day with some simple gratitude.

There was another interesting study, again in 2005, by Leahy, in which scientists found that, a staggering 85% of our worries never actually come true. And for the 15% that do materialise, well, 79% of people found they could handle the situation better than expected or learn something valuable from it. So, in the end, about 97% of what we stress over is just our minds playing tricks on us, exaggerating the threats and misinterpreting reality. These unnecessary worries really amp up the stress levels, leaving you tense and drained, both mentally and physically.

We have limited thinking patterns, like feelings of self-doubt or comparing ourselves to others who have more than us, which can lead to depression. However, research has consistently found that individuals who are more grateful are less depressed compared to individuals who are less grateful. That's why focusing on gratitude really does require regular practice.[23]

Think about how often your internal dialogue repeats: *I'm so fed up, I'm so tired, I can't do this, I'm exhausted, my life is shit, what's the point, I'm in pain.* It's all negative reinforcement.

What I'm saying is, gratitude isn't just a feel-good thing – it's transformative. It shifts how you see yourself and the world, rewires your brain, and even boosts your physical health.

GRATITUDE EXERCISES

1. Set a reminder to go off throughout your day: every time it goes off, express gratitude. This can be out loud, in your head, or written down. I would highly recommend using the emotion wheel on page 149 to help identify the emotion associated with the gratitude you are connecting with. Also, the more detailed the gratitude, the better.

2. Gratitude prompts are perfect for those days when you're feeling a bit stuck or if you're new to this whole gratitude thing.

- Write about someone who makes your life better.
- What do you like most about yourself?
- What things do you use that make life easier?
- Name 3-5 friendships you are grateful for; these can be online or in-person.
- Write about a recent obstacle you faced and how you overcame it.
- Look around and list 5 things that help you in your day-to-day life.
- What is something that you can do today that people 30 years ago couldn't?
- What aspect of your health do you feel grateful for?
- What was the most enjoyable part of your childhood?

- Write about an achievement that you are most proud of.

- Write about a day when you felt really happy.

- Write 3 quotes that you love.

- Write 3 songs that bring you joy.

3. 3. Write a letter to your body from your soul, and another one from your soul to your body. This was a powerful exercise for me. It was recommended to me and I thought *Sure, I'll give it a go but I can't see it doing anything.* I was very wrong; I saw my body in a whole new light. I've included my letters for you to read if you need some inspiration.

FROM MY SOUL TO MY BODY...

Dear Body,

I know we have a love-hate relationship and sometimes it can seem like I'm angry and hateful towards you, in fact, I even tell you I hate you some days.

Today I am here to rectify this. I am grateful for the good days. For the days that aren't full of tremors and pain. I forgive you for the harder days. I now realise it is all out of our control and we must roll with the punches. I recognise now that you too are fighting every day to bring me as much solace as you can and over the last few years you have done just that with the pain being less, the tremors less aggressive and my mind more with it.

So, today I am here to thank you! Thank you for all you have done for me and I hope we can keep fighting together! This fight is not over but knowing I have you in my corner makes it easier.

Forever grateful,
Your Soul xx

FROM MY BODY FROM MY SOUL...

Dear Soul,

I know we have a to-and-fro relationship but as I recognise the growth and ease that has come over the last few years I'm recognising that I would not be here without you.

Your determination and tenacity have got me through many days where I've questioned if I could make it through one more day. I want to thank you for your humour, compassion, and how much you fight and cheer me on from the sidelines. Your positivity and grace have got me here to this point today and I know that from here on out we are going to work together in unity to make this fight not only easier but more enjoyable...well as enjoyable as this can get.

I look forward to this fight as one and thank you for helping to put the pieces back together again. Bring on the future dear friend.

Strong til the end,
Love, Your Body xx

THE POWER OF THE MIND

Our words are POWERFUL! Did you know that we have the power to physically alter the structure of water without even touching it? Simply through our thoughts or intentions, we can influence the crystalline structure of water. The research of Dr. Masaru Emoto is truly fascinating and, frankly, mind-blowing. The words we speak, or even just think about someone else, can actually change the crystalline structure of their body's water.

Let's not forget that our bodies are composed of approximately 70 percent water. So, if we can influence the structure of water without even touching it, it's important to consider the thoughts and intentions we're putting out into the world.

Dr Emoto captured the effects of vibrational frequencies of frozen water crystals using a powerful microscope with high-speed photography. His experiments focused on exposing water to different words and thoughts (both positive and negative), as well as various types of music. He then froze the samples and examined the frozen crystalline structure to compare to the pre 'treated' water sample (also frozen). You could see how after being exposed to certain words the crystalline structure changed. When exposed to the more positive, loving words or classical music the crystalline structures became more aesthetically pleasing, more uniform and symmetrical, like a snowflake. When exposed to more negative thoughts and words or heavy metal music the structures were not as aesthetically pleasing and the structures look as if they'd fallen apart. I highly recommend reading all about Dr Emoto's work in one of his many books, starting with *The Hidden Messages in Water.*

I believe his work is incredible and invaluable for our children to understand that words are powerful and you can physically harm others with what you say and think about them.

A great experiment is the 'rice experiment', something fun to do with your kids, or just try it for yourself. It's a brilliant demonstration of the power of negative thinking (and conversely, the power of positive thinking). Dr Emoto placed portions of cooked rice into two containers. On one container he wrote 'thank you' and on the other 'you fool'. He instructed school children to say the labels on the jars out loud every day when they passed them by. After thirty days, the rice in the container with positive thoughts ('thank you') had barely changed, while the other ('you fool') was mouldy and rotten. You can watch YouTube videos to see the results of other people trying it.

CHAPTER 21

Yoga

Finally, something I can do

So again, I'll bring you back to where we left off. After three months of being mostly bedridden and on Diazepam I began to move around the house again. I had more energy. I found myself actually getting restless, like I had a desire to try and do something. I hadn't felt like that in such a long time. Every ounce of energy was always reserved for existing and getting through the day. So even though I felt this new sense of capacity for more, I knew I couldn't do much and I had to be very careful in how I chose to use my energy. Constantly existing in an unconscious state of fear, worried that I might overexert myself and revert back to a state of barely moving, barely living. The joys of PEM (post-exertional malaise) – it gives you a fear!

I decided to get a mobility scooter, named Steady Eddie, so I could finally get out of the house when everyone was at work. I loved the idea of feeling fresh air on my skin and in my lungs again, feeling free. I figured this would be a perfect way to do something positive for myself without draining the energy I'd built up. I was now reading self-development books, finding my positive achievements every day, practicing gratitude and mindfulness, and connecting with positive people daily, and I'd asked for help from the doctor. I still had shitty days but they weren't as shitty as they had been.

It seemed like a great idea at the time but I ended up not using Steady Eddie all that much due to the vibrations of the road making my body tense up. By the time I got back to the house it would set the tremors off and I'd be exhausted once again. I sometimes had the same thing happen when I was in a car for too long, which meant I didn't want to go far when I did leave the house.

I found myself, as I did most days, scrolling on Instagram and came across a lady with M.E. who did yoga from her bed. I'd already seen Salli had started yoga at home so I figured I could give that a go. Salli recommended Yoga With Adriene on YouTube; she had some great gentle and short yoga practices. It quickly became my favourite thing to do. My arms were surprisingly strong from all the crawling and pulling my dead weight up the stairs. Sometimes I wonder if I could even manage that now. Looking back, I wonder, *How did I not break?* But truth be told, I did break – many times. It's just that I didn't recognize it back then because I was so dissociated. My mind and body simply did what they needed to in order for me to survive.

Yoga was the first form of exercise that my body allowed me to do without consequences (or, at least, minimal consequences). Some days I felt tired after but it would pass by the next day. Not like everything else I'd tried before, where I'd suffer with a flare-up of all symptoms for at least a week, sometimes up to a month.

I felt so much stronger in myself; not just physically but also mentally. There was a clarity, an inner strength and hope that had begun brewing deep inside me, setting that little light of hope ablaze. I generally felt healthier, and my confidence began to grow.

Research has demonstrated yoga's effectiveness in helping survivors of trauma find relief.[24] Another study found that 'isometric yoga as an add-on therapy is both feasible and successful at relieving the fatigue and pain of a subset of therapy-resistant patients with CFS.'[25] 'Yoga also increased vagal nerve function and changed blood biomarkers in a pattern that suggested anti-stress and anti-inflammatory effects', was the conclusion of a study from 2018.[26]

Yoga helped me realise I had been breathing incorrectly. I lay in savasana (corpse pose, my favourite pose) and was instructed to inhale – expanding the stomach like a balloon – and exhale – deflating the balloon. It felt so wrong to me, as I had been doing it the wrong way round all those years. Previously, on my exhale, I expanded the stomach, and when inhaling, I deflated it. I had to use so much focus to consciously control my breath because if I wasn't focusing on it, I would switch right back to the old way.

The way you breathe can profoundly influence your mind, body, and spirit. It might sound unbelievable, but your breath is your life force energy – I truly believe it serves as the pathway to your mind, body, and spirit, like a direct door to accessing truth. When your breathing isn't flowing naturally, it can lead to a misalignment of your mind, body, and spirit. There's a great book by Patrick McKeown called *The Breathing Cure: Develop New Habits for a Healthier, Happier, and Longer Life* if you want to explore the mechanics of breathing further.

Healthy breathing during rest should involve inhaling through the nose, driven by the diaphragm, and exhaling through the nose, even while sleeping. This is our natural breathing rhythm, but life's experiences can lead us to alter our breathing, even from infancy. However, by breathing correctly, you can enhance focus, concentration, posture, and sleep quality, while reducing anxiety and restoring ease to your breathing and, consequently, your life. Proper breathing can also provide support for the spine.

Slow, deep breathing has been shown to activate stretch receptors in the lungs, which influence electrochemical signals in the brain to increase parasympathetic nervous system activity.[27] Deep breathing has been shown to increase heart rate variability, a common indicator and measurement of how well the autonomic nervous system is able to respond and regulate itself in response to changes in the environment.[28] Slow, deep breathing has thus been shown to have a regulating effect on the nervous system.[29]

BREATHING EXERCISE

- Lie on your back on the floor, legs slightly wider than hip-width apart, with one hand on your belly and the other on your heart.
- Take a long, slow inhale through your nose, expanding your belly. Notice how your hand rises with the expansion of the belly.
- Exhale the breath at a steady and slow pace. Notice your hands falling back down.
- Repeat for 10 breaths, or as long as you feel you need to
- Focus only on the rise and fall of your hands on your belly
- Notice how you feel after, compared to when you began

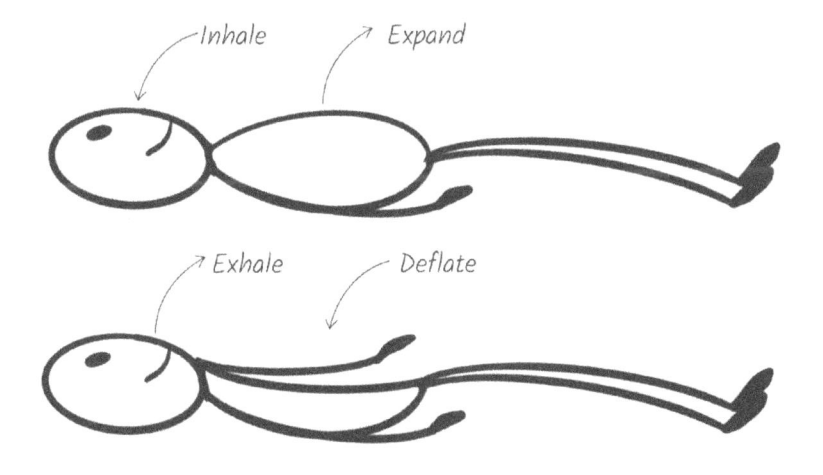

CHAPTER 22
Meditation
Well, I wasn't expecting that

Why meditate? Because it can increase PSNS activity which helps bring a dysregulated nervous system back into balance. There are signs of greater relaxation in the body and a calmer state of mind following meditative practice.[30] There is research to suggest that long-term practice of meditation or mindfulness can result in sustained changes to the ANS.[31]

There are many studies proving that meditation can have a profound impact on your mental, physical and emotional health, and some experience spiritual benefits, too. I wasn't into the spiritual side when I started. It was purely to focus on calming my mind. In fact, when I started, I wouldn't have known what 'spiritual benefits' meant.

Meditating is a super simple practice to take up and doesn't use any energy: you don't even have to sit, you can do it lying down. Whereas you can practise mindfulness whenever and wherever, meditation is a more structured, dedicated practice. Mindfulness can be considered a form of meditation (at least, I feel like it is). Both complement each other beautifully and you may find meditations called 'mindfulness meditation' as well as other types such as a guided meditations.

I believe that finding a balance of the mind, body and spirit will unlock your truth, allowing you to come back to wholeness. It is all interconnected: if one falls out of balance you will find another quickly follows.

I did a little bit of meditating when I started yoga. I didn't know that's what I was doing, though: it was just a peaceful part at the end of the yoga practice. I didn't consciously find mindfulness and meditation until a few months after I'd started yoga.

I had heard people talking about meditation and how good it was but I didn't think I could do it. Then I figured *I won't know until I try* so I gave it a go and found a peacefulness in it. I would fall in and out of a meditation practice over the years. I'd do it religiously, then nothing for months. Over the years, however, it has become a big part of my life. The benefits have been so profound. It felt like stepping out from a small dark space into a beautiful expansive space. I could see through the trees, through the fog, I could see a direction in which to move forward. It helped me to quieten the chaos of my mind and I found a different voice from within: one that was kind, supportive, guiding me to what felt right for me.

I'm not going to lie, at first, I felt so silly and I couldn't sit still at all, opening an eye, scanning the room as if someone was watching me but I kept at it. I would hear other people talk of seeing all these things when they meditated, like the sea or a forest. All I saw was the back of my fucking eyelids; it frustrated me so much. Eventually, I began *watching* the shadows of my eyelids and in time I began to see things, only in a silhouette form but I was excited to finally see something. Once I tried guided meditations, I was well away: someone telling me what to picture was so much easier. I used an app called Headspace, which guided me on how to focus on my breathing to settle myself, then noticing how my body felt and allowing thoughts to flow and actually move past me, not drown me, which I found amazing and naturally wanted to feel this more.

I didn't know it was normal for your mind to wander during meditation. I thought this meant I was doing it wrong. But meditation teaches you to acknowledge the thoughts that arise and then bring your focus back to the breath. You're not doing it wrong and guided meditations can help as you learn.

My mind started to become calmer and it helped me to refocus on what was important for me as a person: not what other people thought, but what I wanted for myself. Do you know how powerful that is?! I'd lived for as long as I could remember in this space of people-pleasing, of second-guessing myself so much that I didn't know which was my own voice any more; it had been overpowered by the one trying to keep me 'safe', constantly mirroring those around me to make them feel comfortable, never speaking out, never saying what I believed in case it caused a conflict. Like I say, it's a powerful practice and for me a life-changing shift. If you suffer with anxiety or depression then I can't recommend this practice enough.

It can be as simple as taking two minutes out of your day. When starting out, start with two to ten minutes a day. It is about finding what works for you, experimenting with different types. Each day might look different, because each day you and your energy are different. I tried lots of different ways: some days I would sit cross-legged and listen to a guided meditation; other times I'd lie on the floor with soothing music; other days I didn't want any music, just silence. Then there were some days when I'd do a yoga practice, fully focusing on my breathing.

Eventually, when I could go for walks again, I started practicing mindfulness while walking (no, I did not walk with my eyes closed, although I have tried that too as a perception exercise – just me playing around and experimenting to better understand myself).

During this time, we moved out of my mum's and in with my dad. After a year with my mum, it all became too much for her working full-time, having the kids there and me being, well, 'useless' is how I felt. I honestly don't know how she managed that long, to be honest.

Since my dad was now retired, he was home to look after me and the kids more, so we moved in with him for a few months. If you saw us together you would never have guessed we had, had a rough past together. We were thick as thieves, laughing all the time, joking and just being awesome. He was also very supportive with my network marketing business and helped me with recipes.

He lived in a farmhouse with a beautiful garden as well as a field, which the kids absolutely loved. We spent more time outside together than I had in years. Living with Dad took a lot of pressure off me, as well as for Lee, in many different ways. Mostly, it was really nice to have someone around during the day to chat and have a laugh with. It just all felt so normal, like a 'proper' father and daughter relationship.

We then moved out of Dad's when we found a bungalow near the kids' school. I was now back doing the school run and it felt like everything I had been working on, to get a balance of good and bad days just flew out the window, leading to a lot of anxiety when leaving the house.

Focusing on my breath with breathing practices from the meditations allowed me to have a new tool that I could use when I was out and about, specifically when picking up the kids from school. There were days when just leaving the house would induce panic – in fact, there were some days when I didn't even have to leave; I just had to think about leaving. This was causing stress hormones to flow through my body, putting me on high alert, readying me to survive the awful, traumatic event of picking up my kids.

I learnt that focusing on my breath allowed me to gain greater control over my tremors, either stopping them from becoming dramatic attention seekers or, if I was really lucky, I'd stop them from appearing at all. My only thoughts were, *Breathe in, breathe out, you've got this ... breathe in, breathe out, no one is looking at you, you've got this ... breathe in, breathe out, you're not going to fall ... breathe in, breathe out, don't look at anyone, no one will talk to you if you don't look at them ... breathe in, breathe out, just get in and get out ... breathe in, breathe out, you've got this.*

There were, however, consequences from the stress that was still flooding my body. I might have been able to get through those moments but once I got home it was like a wave came crashing down on me and sometimes I didn't even make it out of the school car park. The tremors would start so I couldn't drive, it would be so intense and painful that I'd be crying, all while the kids just sat there, waiting to go home.

I'd try and make a joke about it all, put the radio on and sing along to a song, or ask about their day to distract them from the insanity that was taking place. Those times were hard because all I wanted to do was scream and punch things but I didn't want to scare them. So I focused on my breathing (*breathe in, breathe out*) and using the body scan I mentioned earlier I worked through each muscle group in my body, focusing my breath there until my muscles began to relax.

Oh, and it didn't stop there. Once we finally made it home, I would have to get into the house. Luckily, when the kids were there it was much easier; they'd go get my crutches or wheelchair to help me into the house. It breaks my heart as I recall this, that they had to look after me at such a young age, when it wasn't their responsibility to do so.

Again, we would laugh and see the funny side. Honestly, it was all so bloody ridiculous that you couldn't even make it up if you tried. It was like I was living in a comedy film. Especially on the day when Matthew was trying so hard to help me into the wheelchair but hadn't locked the wheel and it started moving away from me just as I used all my strength to haul myself up towards the chair, only to look up and see Isabelle recording the whole thing.

Some days I wasn't so lucky. The days I was on my own, I'd have to drag my carcass across my drive, which I've done more times than I care to admit. When I finally got into the house I'd be completely and utterly exhausted. My whole day became a war to get my body back under control. Some days, the tremors never stopped. Other days, I'd finally make it to the sofa, and after an hour, they would begin to ease off. But, me being me, I'd forget (thanks to disappearing into Netflix), only to then move to get more comfortable and BAM, I'd set the tremors off again. The worst was when I'd been OK for a few hours and think, *I'll make a cuppa now.* I'd get up, start walking and after a few steps I'd crash to the floor like some invisible fucker just tripped me up. There have been a few hard falls on my way to making a cuppa. I finally began putting Zoe the Zimmer or Clive the Crutches next to the sofa so I'd remember I'm not the same person standing up as I am when sitting down.

On these days I would take time to just breathe and focus on my body. The more I did this, the more I noticed my recovery time reduced. All from breathing! And, as I've said before, none of what I was doing was to heal from M.E./CFS, it was just something that I hoped would bring me some peace, something to help me cope with my days a little easier. I never would have guessed it was a stepping stone to a new path opening up for me.

CHAPTER 23

Brainwaves

How is it that meditation can be so powerful? We've spoken about the breath and the innate power that it holds but there is also another reason why meditation is so powerful on the whole being and it is to do with your brainwaves.

What are brainwaves?
Our brain transmits and interprets information through the firing of electrical signals between neurons, or brain cells. These rhythmic patterns of electrical activity are called brainwaves, and we measure them in hertz (Hz). Scientists can track these signals using electroencephalography (EEG) – it's a fancy technique involving putting electrodes on your head to record what's going on up there. The more neurons that are firing, the faster the brainwaves; and when fewer neurons are in action, the frequency slows down.

I learnt about brainwaves about four years after I started meditating, during my studies in sound healing. I didn't have a clue there were different types, each affecting your body and mind in different ways. (I'll explain more about this connection later in the book when I delve into what sound healing entails – as I'm sure you are wondering what sound healing is all about anyway).

There are several distinct types of brainwaves that have been identified, each associated with different states of consciousness, cognitive processes and mental states. The main types of brainwaves are:

Beta waves (12–30 Hz): We are in a beta frequency when we are wide awake. This is normally the state we live in day to day, from the time we wake up until the time we go to sleep. Beta waves are associated with active thinking, focused attention and alertness; your attention is on the external, physical realities. They are present when the brain is engaged in cognitive tasks, problem-solving and during periods of stress or high mental activity.

Beta waves are further divided into low beta (12–20 Hz) and high beta (21–30 Hz) frequencies. Low beta can help to increase our mental abilities and IQ and can also increase our focus. High beta is when you are highly alert, but often also anxious. Staying in this state can create chronic stress and anxiety that undermines your immune system, and can lead to many symptoms of ill health and if the beta wave frequency drops too low, it puts you at risk of depression.

Alpha waves (8–12 Hz): Alpha waves are present when the brain is in a relaxed but wakeful state, where you don't process much information: you're awake and experiencing plenty of mental activity, without being particularly stressed about completing a certain task or attending an event.

You are in alpha when you first get up in the morning and just before you go to sleep. When you close your eyes, your brain automatically starts producing alpha waves. This state is associated with light meditation and a state of mental rest.

Alpha is related to a state of calmness, relaxation and a focused but non-aroused state of mind. Creativity, daydreaming and healing are also linked to this frequency. This frequency can help you to overcome stress and phobias. It is sometimes known as the relaxation response and it is why meditation is so helpful in accessing this state.

Theta waves (4–8 Hz): Theta waves are associated with drowsy sleep, daydreaming, deep states of meditation, and peace and calm – all of which promote healing. There are now healing modalities (therapeutic techniques that seek to balance the mind, body, emotions, and spirit) which focus entirely on theta waves. This is because it is easier to identify and change limiting beliefs and patterns in the unconscious mind while in a theta brainwave. In theta, we can access deep creativity and tranquillity.

Rapid eye movement (REM) sleep, extreme relaxation, lucid dreaming and out-of-body experiences can also occur in this state. Theta can also be excellent for hypnosis and accelerated learning.

Delta waves (0.5–4 Hz): Delta waves are the slowest recorded brainwaves in human beings. They are typically associated with deep sleep or dreamless sleep, unconsciousness, and states of physical healing and regeneration.

In these states, our neural processes slow down considerably and you can focus on what you have seen and heard during the day. This is when information you absorbed through your senses during the day is consolidated and information you have collected is stored in your memory.

Gamma waves (above 30 Hz): Although gamma waves are the fastest brainwaves and have the highest frequency, they also seem to be the key to enlightened states of mind and inner peace. They are associated with complex cognitive processing, perception and the integration of information from different brain regions. Gamma waves are believed to be involved in higher-order cognitive functions, learning and conscious awareness.

A study was conducted on eight long-term Tibetan Buddhist practitioners of meditation and, using electrodes, researchers monitored the patterns of electrical activity produced by their brains as they meditated. The researchers compared the brain activity of the monks to a group of novice meditators.

The study showed the monks had a significant increase in brain activity in the left prefrontal cortex, the part of the brain associated with self-control, happiness and compassion. It also showed reduced activity in the amygdala – the brain's fight-or-flight centre. This suggests that meditation can make you happier and more compassionate.

In a normal meditative state, both groups were shown to have similar brain activity. When the monks were asked to focus on feelings of compassion, their brains immediately moved into the gamma frequency in a rhythmic and coherent pattern, suggesting neuronal structures were firing in harmony. In contrast, the novice meditators produced very few, if any, gamma waves. However, with further practice, a number of rhythmic signals did appear to strengthen in beginner meditators, implying that producing gamma wave rhythms is a skill that can be learnt through training.[32]

According to neuroscientists, people can train themselves to increase their gamma frequency. In fact, by focusing on compassion and love, you can increase your gamma output.

Meditating tips
1. Don't over complicate it
2. Start with 2 minutes and build up
3. Do it when you wake up (before getting out of bed) or last thing at night before you fall asleep
4. If you're struggling to relax, try moving your eyes to look up about 45 degrees while they are closed. I find this helpful for relaxing the muscles in my face and shoulders

Head to www.hope-light.co.uk/bookresources where you will find a selection of meditations to try out for yourself.

CHAPTER 24

Mitochondrial Therapy

Game changer

Some time in 2016 a friend suggested a book called *Diagnosis and Treatment of Chronic Fatigue Syndrome: It's Mitochondria Not Hypochondria!* by Dr Sarah Myhill. This was the first book I read that finally explained what was happening inside my body at a cellular level. Explaining what could be causing the fatigue and why resting like 'normal' people doesn't recharge those with chronic fatigue at the same rate and how we can 'borrow' energy only to then have to pay it back with interest.

Mitochondria are the powerhouses of cells; they are what generate energy, similar to a battery. They convert food into an energy source that can be easily used by the cell, called adenosine triphosphate (ATP). Studies are finding that M.E./CFS patients have a lower production of ATP, compared to that of healthy people.[33] Poor ATP formation means less energy for your cells, causing them to slow down, which in turn means your bodily functions struggle. This would explain M.E./CFS symptoms such as fatigue, brain fog and muscle pain.

I began Googling Sarah Myhill (like you do) as she mentioned in her book that she does tests and works with those with CFS. Unfortunately, she was no longer taking on any more patients. My hope dashed once again. Mind you, at least I'd finally found something to explain what was happening, with a scientific explanation behind it and which could provide something other than *Your bloods are within normal range so there's nothing wrong with you.* My spirit felt so uplifted after reading her book, again feeding that spark of hope.

Luckily, the universe plays its own game and when you are open to receiving, it will bring you what you need at the time you need it. I had mentioned Sarah Myhill's book to Salli before she had gone away for a work convention. When Salli got back, she messaged to say she'd been talking to the photographer at the event about M.E./CFS and he mentioned that he had just become a practitioner in mitochondrial therapy! She couldn't believe it and neither could I. It was clearly a sign.

It was different to the testing I had read about in the book, but I didn't care as long as it was working with mitochondria. Research-mode switched on once more, I gathered all the information and facts on the doctor behind the creation of this programme, Dr Kučera. I read the entire website (it was an easy layout which really helped with my brain fog) and watched all the videos on there. Then I Googled for more and YouTubed him so I could learn more about the process.

The treatment itself was to take supplements that he had designed: the amount you took depended on the results the heart rate variability (HRV) test showed. It was completely tailored to your body's needs to help it function properly once again.

The test itself looked incredibly simple: electrodes were placed on the wrists and ankles, which were hooked up to a computer. The software then takes the information it receives from the electrodes (because we are electrical beings) to provide information on how well your nervous system is functioning. It couldn't be any simpler: just sit still for five minutes.

About a year after the doctor's appointment with the doctor who listened, I booked an appointment with the mitochondrial practitioner Salli had told me about, who was called Steve. He had trained under Dr Kučera and his team. My mum, as always, was by my side as I decided to try this out.

I will never forget the look on Steve's face when he saw my results. There is a scoring system to the tests, providing an overall score between 1 and 10. The higher the number the more out of balance your body is. My results came up as an overall 7. Steve looked at me and said, 'I would never have thought this by looking at you.'

Remember, I had become a master at hiding what was really going on inside: with a nice big smile and a splash of humour you can fool so many people, even yourself! I can't tell you what a relief it was to have evidence that I was not OK, to hold a physical piece of paper that proved I wasn't lying, I wasn't making all this up, that my body was in fact as fucked up as I had suspected and now, I could prove it.

Dr Kučera was part of the team who was responsible for the health and wellbeing of the cosmonauts in the Russian Space Program, including the Mars 500 Project. His research and interest in mitochondrial medicine span over thirty years, which led him to develop a range of very specific nutritional supplements to help repair mitochondria.

These supplements have shown to be effective on the body's nervous system and there have been extraordinary results across a range of disorders, improving heart health as well as supporting immunity and improving stress resilience.

I began taking the supplements Steve recommended alongside the nutritional supplements I'd been taking daily for the past few years. Each new supplement had its own job in repairing the mitochondria. I was told that carnosine was the one for repairing the mitochondria, Q10 enzyme was to bring in energy and the flavonoids were used to sweep away all the by-products of the reactions that were taking place, so essentially you don't have dust clogging up any free areas.

Within a month I began playing with my kids more and I wasn't feeling as tired as I used to after doing things. I also found myself waking up at 6.30am, which was unheard of for me. I was just wide awake and ready to go for the day. I also did more chores around the house. Things that would have taken me all week to get through now only took a couple of days. I was able to increase my yoga practice and wash my hair on the same day, which had been unheard of for nearly a decade. We even went on our first family holiday abroad and I remember it all just being so bloody easy. If anything, I found myself feeling restless, wanting to do more.

However, after a couple of months of enjoying this energy boost, I started to struggle again, and over the next three months the fatigue got a lot worse. I spoke to Steve during those weeks, and we adjusted my supplements, but nothing seemed to help. If anything, I felt worse, and after another test, my overall score was still 7, with my heart rate even higher at 104 bpm (60-75 bpm being the norm). Steve spoke to the lady who'd trained him and they recommended I see Dr Kučera himself, as he was the only one who could run tests on the heart. The test for the heart was the same as normal, I assume it was just different software used specifically for checking the heart.

I went to London for the test as I was going on holiday (again) with Salli. She came with me for the test. They repeated the HRV test I'd had done a month earlier. My overall score was now an 8. I was worse, and my resting heart rate was now 118bpm. However, feeling like this turns out to be normal for most people, especially those who have suffered for a long time. Your body goes through so many changes at a cellular level that it is bound to be felt by the body, a bit like a detox. After so many years of suffering I needed to be patient for my body to heal, to repair, to do what it needed.

I don't know what I expected when it came to my heart but I can tell you I didn't expect to hear 'You'll be lucky if this heart lasts you another five to ten years.'

My reaction was along the lines of giggling and saying 'Oh, alright', because how do you respond to that? Internally a storm was beginning to swirl but I wouldn't let myself feel it, not yet. I was at Salli's and we were going away in a few days. Now was not the time to let myself think about it. Of course, I did think about, constantly, I just didn't talk about it.

I rang my mum to let her know my results, but I couldn't really speak about it. I kept it short as I choked down my tears because I knew I was on the edge of breaking; she probably knew it too.

It happened that at this time I saw my friend's post about how they had all gone out together with their partners, and in that moment, I felt hurt by them. I knew it was silly because I wasn't even home to go out with them, but not knowing about their plans made me feel left out, rejected, alone, and insignificant. All perfectly normal emotions to feel. However, as I was already feeling alone, insignificant, and rejected, even by my own heart, I unconsciously attached to the next thing that provoked the same feelings in me.

At the same time, however, I knew this moment was coming: we'd been drifting apart for a while and I can hold my hands up and say I wasn't always a good friend and would describe myself as a bit of a bitch at times. There are many things I'd love to take back, to say and do but that's part of life, part of growing up. We learn from our mistakes and we do better next time.

I also know now that I was never really myself around them, or anyone for that matter, not truly. I always wanted to be accepted, so I wore the mask I knew so well. I know I hurt their feelings at times, as they did mine – not that I knew how to express this. I didn't want to lose the only friends I had left – let's not forget, I didn't actually know how to communicate back then.

So, feeling all this on top of everything else I was feeling (or trying not to feel), I broke and cried my little heart out to Salli. I just felt so much guilt, shame, fear and grief all at once.

When I got back from the holiday, I was put on beta-blockers in the hope they would help reduce my heart rate so my heart could finally begin repairing itself.

I continued to see Dr Kučera and Sherri (Steve's teacher) every few months, which was a four-hour drive away. My mum accompanied me and we ended up making them into mother-daughter getaways, finding cute little places to stay.

I couldn't have done this treatment without my mum and dad. I couldn't afford to do it myself, especially now I had to up the carnosine dosage to help my heart and the rest of my body. I needed twice as much as I did before, but my god it was worth it.

I could finally understand and explain the difference between 'fatigue' and 'tired'. Tired is when you can push through and still feel good after or take a nap and feel recharged. Fatigue is when your body feels like it's made from lead and you can feel every muscle in your body when you try to move. A bit like being the person on the bottom of a dog pile and trying to move so you can breathe.

I began walking: actually walking, outside, in the fresh air, listening to birds and feeling the wind and rain on my face. Even to this day I appreciate the feel of wind and rain on my skin. After so many years of rarely being able to get outside you realise just how much you take for granted every day. Not just being outside but simple acts of getting dressed, standing to make a cup of tea, washing yourself in the bath, getting yourself downstairs.

I started walking with my mum, as a safety precaution. We didn't know if this would last, if I would overdo something and my legs would just crumple beneath me, like they'd done so many times in the past. There was a constant underlying worry, like waiting for the other shoe to drop.

I went back to Dr Kučera after 5 months, who took another look at my heart. I couldn't believe it; the difference was more than I expected. The heart imagery was nearly all green, whereas before huge areas of red were visible (image below). The relief was astronomical.

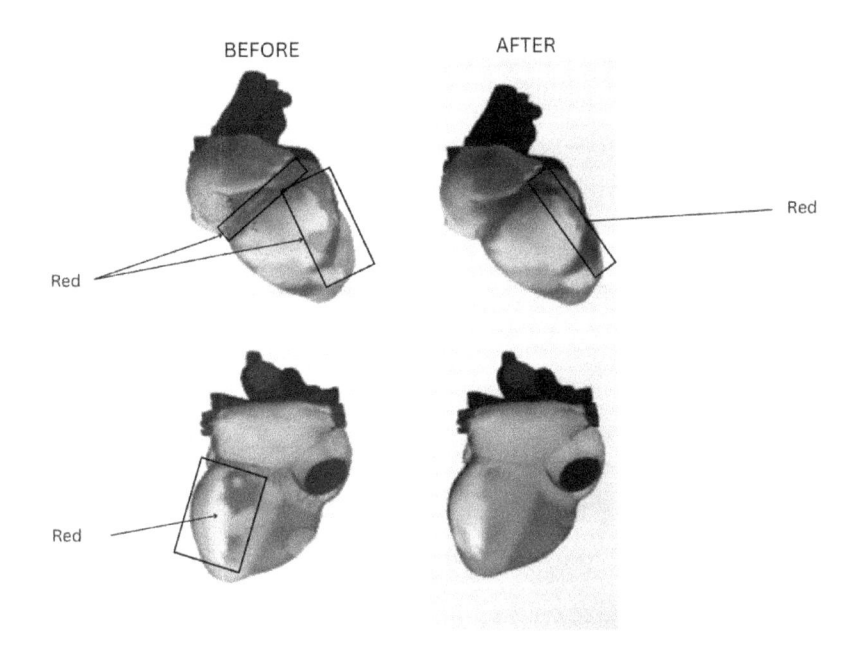

Image 1: First heart scan (left) vs second heart scan (right)

About 3 months after seeing Dr Kučera initially (June 2017), I began walking on my own as my energy levels were back up, my overall score was back up to a 5 and I was becoming restless. I'd drop the kids off at school and drive somewhere for a walk. I had to find flat walks to build up my strength and as I lived on a hill there was no way I was attempting that yet, especially on my own.

When I started walking on my own, I kept crying, all the time. I was just in this constant state of awe and disbelief. I didn't think I'd ever be able to do this again. To have this independence. I'd be OK for a few steps, then another wave of emotion would wash over me. I must have looked like a right idiot to anyone who passed or they must have assumed I was having a rough day when in actual fact they were witnessing a miracle.

In true Katie style, I *did* overdo it! I relapsed: the tremors got worse, and twelve months after starting the mitochondria programme, I was back to being in and out of the wheelchair and my overall score dropped back down to a 7. My god, I could have kicked myself. I was too cocky.

I knew I had to start again, take everything at a much slower pace and check in regularly with myself to see how I was really doing. I struggled with another bout of depression during this period. I just felt so stupid, and really beat myself up for it.

Once again, however, I'd improve for a few months and I'd crash again. This became a familiar cycle for the next couple of years. I just couldn't seem to get any consistency with any of it. Don't get me wrong, I was still doing better than I used to, and life was much more manageable, but I wanted something I could rely on: I wanted more. I was still in and out of a wheelchair at times and not able to leave the house on my own much, plus the anxiety was getting out of control.

It's hard to explain, but at this time I was better but not better. The severity of the symptoms was less, I had more good days than bad days and my recovery time was much quicker, but I also still had tremors, fatigue and pain on the bad days. Sometimes I'd go days, even weeks feeling pretty good but equally I could have bad days and weeks of bad days where I'd want to scream until I had no voice left, throw things until I physically couldn't move my body any more. It was very up and down, but overall better; my quality of life had improved.

I was getting what I had set out for: more energy so I could be around my kids more. This was the turning point of starting to feel like a mum again. Feeling present with them, instead of trying to survive.

CHAPTER 25

Awakening

How is this possible?

For some of you this may be an eye-rolling section and for some of you, you'll know exactly what I'm talking about. Or maybe this is the moment your mind begins to get curious and connects with a part of you that believes in something, you just don't know what 'it' is. All of these are perfectly normal places to be in. I have been all versions of the above along my journey, so just meet yourself where you are right now. I am not asking you to believe in what I share: it is simply my experience and my truth. You will find your own as we move forward.

'Awakening' is when you suddenly feel like you've woken up (obviously!). It is commonly used in the spiritual sense, like you have woken up from a deep sleep and suddenly see life, possibilities and connections in a whole new light. Finding answers that eluded you before, understanding what you couldn't quite fathom before. You wake up from the monotony, the autopilot version of your life. A bit like someone flicking a switch and suddenly a bright light comes on, showing you something beautiful and new, something that touches your soul, waking it up. You begin to find a belief in something bigger than yourself, a trust you didn't have before, a knowing.

For some this can happen after massive events like near death-experiences, or life-threatening and life-changing situations. For others, like me, it's through baby steps; little 'aha!' moments, like a door opening, finding something new, only to find another door, discovering a bit more, then another door and another and with each one, your belief and trust in the divine rises and strengthens. I personally use the term divine, but there are various terms like God, universe, and others used interchangeably. Feel free to choose whichever resonates most with you.

My awakening was the beginning of something new, a place where I discovered so much, especially when it came to healing modalities. Up until this point I had just been trying 'normal' things. Things that made sense to my mind and were socially accepted by others. However, finding my spiritual side is what opened up a whole new world to me and ultimately led me to truly heal myself. What I want to emphasise yet again, though, is I had no intention of trying to heal: it was just pure curiosity. They say curiosity killed the cat but my curiosity helped me gain my entire life back. I just had to go against the grain of what had been taught to me as a child as 'normal'.

I discovered a lot in a relatively short time (as you'll see by how much is packed into the next few chapters). Learning one healing modality and then another, learning how to connect to spirit and myself. I was addicted to learning and I wanted to know everything.

Being an incredibly sceptical person, I needed baby steps into the world of spirituality. I needed to process and adjust to what I was learning and discovering about myself and the world of spirituality. I also think I was in such a delicate and sensitive place that a big awakening would likely have knocked me backwards – that or I was just way too stubborn to accept what was right in front of me. My mind loves facts, logic and research so it would always be a challenge for that part of myself to trust and believe in something that I couldn't see with my physical eyes.

A part of me had always believed in 'something', but I had no idea what it was. Religions never felt right: I couldn't understand why there were so many different ones when I had always felt they all come down to the same thing. That everything is connected; beliefs don't need to be segregated and certainly shouldn't be used against anyone to belittle or shame them. We are all human beings. I've never really understood why we can't see each other as such. I've had this feeling ever since I was a child, I just didn't know how to explain this big feeling.

I would also find myself triggered by the word 'God', which comes from the imagery stored in my mind of an old dude with a white beard who lives in the sky. It felt too small to describe what I felt. What I felt was so much bigger, so expansive. I've never shared this before now as I was worried about what people would think, and I worry about offending people. Then, I remember that other people's beliefs and opinions are not my own, and they do not define me. This is my truth, my belief and I am safe to share them. This is a book of truth and authenticity after all.

I felt this massive connection more when I was a child than I ever did as a teenager, though I have always held a firm belief that everything happens for a reason. I have always felt like there is something around me, supporting me in my hardest times. I suppose it's why I went to see a psychic medium in the first place. Curiosity, and something within me that wanted to know there's more to this life.

When my nan-nan (my dad's mum) passed away in 2013, I had an experience that has never left me. I remember my dad telling me she'd passed and what time she'd passed; I froze for a few seconds because I had looked at the clock at that exact time that day.

A day or so later, I was working at my jewellery table (beneath the front room window) when a bird came and started tapping its beak against the glass. I smiled and thought, *That's cute*. Then it came back every day to tap on the window and I just had this overwhelming feeling that it was my nan-nan. I'd speak to her and it was like I could feel her standing behind me. After her funeral, the bird never came back. The whole encounter felt so powerful.

On days when I felt sad I found myself talking to my nan-nan, as I always had this sense that she was there, especially when I was driving (I spent a lot of time crying in the car: it was my safe place to feel everything I felt I had to hide from everyone else).

I have always had a habit of speaking out loud, as if I am talking to someone. It's a great way for me to figure stuff out: it's as if my head is too jam-packed for any more thoughts so saying them out loud lets me free up some space in my head. There has always been that belief that I was being watched over, that someone was always right by my side, even if I wasn't actually thinking it at the time.

I had a few experiences as a kid that raised questions, especially in one of the army bases where we lived. My things would be moved around in my room at night, which used to freak me out. There was a time I was riding my bike on the road and I heard someone shout my name, but there was no one else around. I told my mum about this recently and she asked if I was doing something dangerous. I laughed and said 'I was riding my bike with no hands.' And my mum looked at me as if to say *That explains it.*

And don't even get me started on the middle room in my mum's house. I've spent many a night in there sleeping with my light on. There were just so many little things that happened, but nothing was scarier than sleeping, turning over in bed and opening my eyes to see a grey wispy male face staring right at me, a few inches from my face. (Just like when you have kids and they stand right by the bed saying nothing, but stay where they are, watching you sleep, waiting for you to open your eyes, making you jump out your skin and halfway across the bed). I spent months sleeping with the light on after that.

When Isabelle was a baby she had that same middle room and every night she stood in her cot crying and crying until she eventually threw up ... every night! We never had that problem in any other house or if we went away somewhere: just in that middle room. She would also be pointing to the cupboard. Not scary at all, right?

So, there were all these things as I grew up, yet there was still that part of me who was super logical, analytical and needed evidence. The reason I couldn't surrender to fully believing was because I was so worried about what others would think about me.

I only went to the psychic medium the first time because my mum had been with a friend at work and she thought she was brilliant. When my mum suggested I should go, my curiosity was piqued and I decided to give it a go, just to see what she said. I went in 2009, when I was pregnant with Isabelle. I was so sceptical and didn't want to give any information about myself so I would only say yes or no, which makes me laugh and I roll my eyes now.

My sceptical side couldn't understand how it was possible, but another part of me was thinking, *YES, this is going to be amazing.* When we arrived, my first thoughts were, *Ooh, this is fancy.* They had a gated drive, which I always associate with wealth. As I walked in, I was greeted by their dog and the woman's partner in their open and airy foyer. I didn't have to wait; I went straight in to see the psychic medium. It was just a little office type room in the house, with a desk, a bookcase and two chairs. The lady was lovely and so normal. I think I was expecting there to be tie-dye fabrics everywhere, incense burning and floaty music but no, it was just a normal lady with a bubbly, warm, inviting energy, dressed in smart casual clothes. I took a seat and proceeded to do my best to give nothing away.

She connected with Nanny Morna (my mum's mum) and told me quite a few things that had my jaw dropping in just a few minutes. I remember her saying that my nan had sent Lee to me, which makes sense now because we ended up getting married on my nan and gramps's anniversary date. We had originally planned our wedding for 10 October 2010 so we could have 10.10.10 as our anniversary, but the universe had other plans and it ended up being 9 October, which my mum later told me was Nan and Gramps' anniversary. That felt like my nan saying *See, I told you.*

I couldn't believe how accurate this medium was with all the things she said. Then the things she predicted came true. She was accurate with so much – even the speeding ticket my hubby was going to get! (I warned him about it too, and he still got it). I went to this psychic medium three times over the space of about seven years.

Now I can't tell you how or why, as I have no recollection of the thought process in purchasing or where I bought them from, but I must have decided to buy a tarot deck in 2018. I had no idea how to use them; I'd just pull cards for myself and then read the meaning of the card in the booklet that came with it.

I kept getting the death card – which means there's a cycle of my life coming to an end, not an actual death. I sensed it. I knew it was true, but I couldn't see how or what it meant for my future. At this point, I felt myself drifting away from the network marketing job I'd joined in 2015, and I also wasn't making silver jewellery anymore.

During this time, suddenly someone appeared on Facebook: another psychic medium, Anna, and I thought, *Fuck it, let's see if she can shine some light on what is going on.* As with so many other points in my life, I'm not really sure how it came about, but I'm glad it did as it turned out to be the best reading I had ever had; I was crying within two minutes. She picked up all my anxiety, worries and she connected with my nan-nan. Anna described her perfectly and told me things about her that I didn't even know. When I checked them with my dad after and he confirmed them, I was even more gobsmacked.

Anna then asked if I had tarot and oracle cards and I laughed and told her I'd recently bought some but had no clue what I was doing. She recommended a few decks that were easier to start with than the one I had. I bought them straight after our call, along with some crystals, because, well, it would be rude not to, right? Anna had also said she saw me doing readings for other people. I couldn't see that being a thing, but she said anyone can learn to read cards and, again, I just felt it, I believed her. It was like getting permission for an ordinary person like me, who had no idea about anything spiritual, to find their own guidance.

Anna said my nan-nan was around me all the time and she would help me with the cards. I had rarely felt her around me at this point but after that reading, I felt her so strongly whenever I picked up the cards. It's hard to explain but you know that feeling when someone is looking over your shoulder? It was like that. You know when you can't actually see them but you know 100 per cent that they are there, like there is a weight, pressure, energy pushing against you. That is what it feels like when I connect with spirit. It was like I could feel her and hear her voice.

I kept reading for myself and I couldn't believe how much I cried. It just felt so powerful to feel this connection to something, even though I couldn't see it. I felt so much support and so seen because the cards never lie, and my god did they read me dirty some days. Picking up on the shit I hid inside. They were spookily accurate and yet at the same time my mind was having a meltdown because it didn't make sense to my logical side.

I didn't stop there: the universe worked seamlessly and good old Facebook again showed me that Anna was doing a spiritual development course and I just knew, I knew I had to do it, there was no thinking about it. I wanted to learn more, I wanted to read the cards properly.

It was a four-week course, but I was worried about the final week which was mediumship. I said I wouldn't do that week as I didn't want to connect with spirits because it scared me. She encouraged me to just show up and choose if I wanted to participate on the day. I ended up giving it a go and blew my own bloody mind when I connected with *her* nan and got so much right. That was it, I was hooked!

She taught us how to use pictures of people's loved ones to connect with them, so I practised whenever I could, using the ladies in the group who were also learning, and used pictures of my own loved ones and then I went on to Lee's family. It just felt so simple: it really wasn't scary or a complicated process like I had told myself it would be.

I then practised without pictures and used the cards on anyone who would let me. I read for my dad and his wife, and it was bloody brilliant; we couldn't believe the things I picked up. I was so grateful that they let me frequently practise. Hours would go by some days.

I picked a card for Dad one day that said he would be a spiritual teacher and he laughed. I told him what Anna had told me: that everyone can do this, it's just practice and being open to it. He wasn't convinced but eventually I started telling both my dad and his wife everything I knew. They too began practising and we'd all read for each other. We all saw things in different ways, meaning we learnt a lot from each other and had loads of fun, too.

My dad is now a fantastic medium and does a lot of platform work. It honestly blows me away the amount of evidence he is able to pick up from loved ones. When I say evidence, I mean that he is able to obtain accurate information about deceased people without any information from the person who is having the reading. It really is jaw-dropping.

We didn't stop there. I was meditating one day (by this point, my meditation practices had evolved from focusing on the breath and quietening the mind to full-on spiritual journeys), asking spirit what was next for me. All I saw was the word 'reiki' appearing in front of me and then moving closer towards my face. I had no idea what reiki was so I began my usual research routine, after which I knew I wanted to train in it instantly and bought a few books. I looked for someone who taught it in Wales. I eventually decided who I wanted to train with and it wasn't just me; Dad and his wife came too.

I found it absolutely fascinating and I couldn't believe how there were times when the reiki healer wasn't touching my body but I could feel so much in my body. There were times when she was standing at my head but my leg was twitching or my stomach made weird noises. Afterwards, I felt like I'd had a massage, that spa-like daze you get when you're super relaxed and feel completely blissful. It was such a simple thing to do and I knew I wanted to do this for other people, so they could also experience this blissful, uplifting feeling.

Reiki is defined by the Oxford English dictionary as 'a healing technique based on the principle that the therapist can channel energy into the patient by means of touch, to activate the natural healing processes of the patient's body and restore physical and emotional wellbeing.'

large-scale study showed that 'a single session of Reiki improves multiple variables related to physical and psychological health.'[34] Another study compared three groups – reiki, sham reiki (placebo), and standard care – and found that 'only the reiki group showed significant reductions in pain, blood pressure, respiration rate, and state anxiety, providing evidence for a full-scale clinical study.'[35]

In 2018 – the same year I'd bought my first card deck and seen Anna – I started a business doing psychic mediumship readings. After three months of Reiki training, I added Reiki; three months after that, I added aromatherapy massage. There wasn't much thought put into creating this business; I just dived straight in because I knew this was when I was supposed to do it.

Those cards never did lie: it was like a shedding of my old self and I began to embrace this new spiritual path. Mentally and emotionally I was feeling the best I'd felt in such a long time; stable for the first time in years.

Of course, my sceptical, logical side struggled and I had so many moments where I thought I must be making this up, how it can't be possible! However, the feedback from others always put my mind at ease and it reminded me to just trust what was happening and stop over-thinking.

I became addicted to learning everything I could about the spiritual world. I started learning about chakras, which still fascinate me, then crystals, completing my level 1 crystal healing course. I knew when I finished the course that crystals would be an additional healing modality integrated into my reiki sessions, not separate from. I learnt about the meaning of colours and angels and in time I learnt numerology, too. I use the meanings of colours and numbers every day and I am always working with angels. It's a constant in my life, even when I'm not feeling 'spiritual'.

In respect to where I was with M.E./CFS, I was up and down. Things were slightly better, but I continued to have setbacks and physical symptoms. I was still having days where I'd be crawling into the house from the school run, or walking in the kitchen and boom, legs would decide to clock off early. But as an overview, I *was* better: not healed, not cured, not whole, but better. My quality of life was improving, my energy levels were better, my pain was not as severe as it used to be. It was what I'd been hoping for when I started out on my journey of alternative practices.

The funny thing is, when you get what you want, it's never enough. Now I wanted more. Now I wanted less pain again, fewer tremors and spasms, less anxiety, less fatigue. So my search for more continued.

CHAPTER 26

Sound Healing

Shit! That was powerful

About a year after becoming a reiki practitioner, I found myself once again looking into something that caught my attention, having no idea what it was or how it worked. This time it was 'sound healing', which I discovered through a spiritual course I was taking, run by a healer called Rakaiel. I loved how the course strengthened my connection to myself and I noticed I developed a deeper sense of knowing, of trust within myself. Rakaiel is a sound practitioner and she had these incredible crystal singing bowls that I became obsessed with listening to. There was just something that called to me and I instantly knew it was something I had to learn how to do for myself.

While I looked for the right course to become a sound healing practitioner, I knew I needed to have more experience with sound healing as a client. I was at a spiritual fair where my dad was doing readings and I was helping a friend out on his stall. I noticed the fair had a gong sound bath later in the day so I thought, *Perfect, this is a great opportunity to experience some sound healing.*

Before heading over to the room my legs had become painful and extremely heavy from standing at the stall all day – they hurt so much I nearly didn't go into the hall because it seemed too far to walk (100m). My dad encouraged me to go, so I did. I came out of that room feeling like I was walking on air: it was so easy to move my legs, and I was so relaxed and at ease. It was at this point I fell in love with sound and the possibilities it held for helping others. I'd only experienced thirty minutes with a group of people and my body felt like it could breathe again. I could only imagine what a one-to-one session might do!

I went on a hunt to find a local sound practitioner. I wanted to try a one-to-one session before booking the training – mostly because it was a big investment and I wanted to make sure I wasn't wasting my money. (Though really, I'd already made my mind up when I had the gong bath at the fair).

I booked a session with a local practitioner and, well, it was OK. I don't know what I was expecting, but it didn't quite match what was in my mind. I think I was expecting a spa-type set-up, all light and airy, but it was in a small darkish room in the back of someone's house. Although the session itself was relaxing and calming, and I did feel lighter leaving, I couldn't help but feel a little disappointed. I don't know why, it wasn't like I was expecting sparks to fly out of my arse or a rainbow to explode from my head! It just felt a bit 'meh' and I think it was mostly because I struggled to really relax and switch my mind off because my mind was racing with thoughts like *Ooh what instrument is she using now? Oh, I felt something twitch. Where is she standing now? Fuck, my feet are cold.* And when she used her voice, well, I was just not prepared for it, I didn't know that was a part of sound healing, which is quite ridiculous if you think about it. Internally, I was doing everything I could not to laugh out loud.

In spite of this experience, that gong bath really stuck with me and I was still determined to become a practitioner. In the end, it took me about six months to decide where and how to study. I took a hybrid course, both online and in-person learning, which suited me perfectly as the in-person part was in Wales. Like all the things I've ever tried, I didn't have much in the way of expectations; I just followed what I felt was right.

Before I even started the training, I bought a crystal singing bowl, because why not. I was fascinated with the sounds it created, so I bought a new one any time I had some spare money. Then for the course itself I bought a starter kit: three Tibetan singing bowls, three tuning forks and a rattle.

MY SOUND PRACTITIONER EXPERIENCE

The training days were all about learning how to play a whole range of instruments, it was absolutely brilliant. It also included the voice. Using my voice made me feel so self-conscious, I couldn't sing for shit. I had always been the quietest one in a group setting so no one could hear me, or I would mime the words. Very different from when I was on my own in my car or drunk.

Day one: we were chanting and I was here to learn so I gave it a go, albeit a very self-conscious go. Then something happened. Everyone was chanting and the sound of the twelve people chanting hit something inside me that made me burst into tears. I had to stop chanting because I was crying so much. It was just so powerful; like a dam had burst open and there was no stopping it. The intensity of emotions was like being pummelled by a wave. I wanted to wail, to scream, to cry out but then I remembered where I was, already feeling self-conscious and silly, so I did everything I could to block that dam back up.

Luckily, everyone else had their eyes closed so I pulled myself together by the end of the chanting and at the end I just mentioned that 'my eyes leaked', not that I'd experienced something that still to this day I have no words to describe it. This was the day I learnt the power of the voice. Something we all own – and bonus, it's free.

The closest thing I've found to experiencing this again is listening to chant music. I do this when I feel I need a good shaking to my core, because that is what it feels like. Your whole body vibrates so deeply that it almost undoes you. Shaking any shit you've been carrying for too long so you can finally let it move through and out of you.

I have since learnt that it doesn't matter what sound comes out of you: the sound that emerges is actually the exact sound, vibration and frequency that you need in that moment. Our bodies have their own intelligence, they know what we need far more than we know consciously. The more you surrender to it, the more powerful and healing it is.

This is something I've had to practise because I feel so silly using my voice. That inner critic is always telling me how shit I sound, that I'm not good enough, that everyone will laugh if they ever heard me. Like most of these beliefs, it comes from a past experience as a child and I held on to that comment, retelling myself that story again and again until it became an absolute truth. I'm still working on undoing this but I have managed to incorporate it into sessions with my clients and sound baths.

At first, I was not interested in the tuning forks; they didn't look like anything special and I just didn't take to them at all. That was until we practised on each other and I was shocked at just how much they affected me; they switched my tense body straight into a relaxed state. Never judge a book by its cover, right? The same goes for instruments: just because they don't look fancy doesn't mean they're not powerful.

I learnt that each instrument had its own unique impression and experience on me as we practised with the variety of instruments. The Tibetan bowls always gave me a grounding, earthing feeling whereas the crystal bowls made me feel so light and had an ethereal feeling to them. The drums always take me to my ancestors and bring in strong rooted vibes. The gong, however, surprised me the most.

It was the third day of training and my body was starting to fatigue from being away from home, from concentrating, from socialising, from my inner critic constantly appearing and telling me shit about myself. On this day, as we practised on each other I could feel myself relaxing which was lovely, until it felt like the tremors and spasms were brewing under my skin, which is the weirdest sensation: a mix between a thousand ants under the skin and pins and needles coming from deep inside the body, slowly making their way to the surface, like a volcano readying to erupt.

As the student waved the gong over me it was like my whole body took a massive breath in and let out the biggest sigh, and just like that the volcano quietened right back down and those weird sensations just vanished. In that moment I knew this was some powerful shit! I have never been able to stop tremors once they get to the ants and pins and needle sensations. If I was lucky enough to know they were arising I would find somewhere to sit or lie down until they passed, if they passed. You can imagine why I didn't leave the house much, especially on my own. That day when I first experienced the gong, however, I was perfectly fine for the rest of the day and I didn't even have the same fatigue at the end of the day like I'd had the previous two days.

After the course I began exploring sound even more, learning as much as I could. Everything I learnt was just fascinating. I immersed myself in the world of tuning forks and found someone called Eileen Day McKusick whose work with tuning forks helped me to really understand the body and how emotions become stored within the body.

What's more, how those emotions become stored in specific areas of the body, categorising themselves.

I did a few more courses, workshops and masterclasses so I could learn even more. I wanted to know how sound worked, how it travelled through the body, how it interacted with our energies. And then how to use it to help others to heal.

There is still so much more to learn but like anything, it takes time. When it comes to tapping into the forces of the unseen (well, unseen to the physical eyes) it takes time to learn the language. And this language is your own unique language. It is yours, and yours alone, only you can decipher and learn it. You can learn from other people talking about how they communicate with themselves, but it ultimately comes down to your own experiences and, as always, trial and error. Reconnecting to your intuition is like strengthening a muscle. The more you work it, the easier it is and the stronger it becomes.

When I began introducing sound into my other modality practices with my clients, such as reiki and aromatherapy massage, they all said the same. It was like the sessions were upgraded: they felt even more relaxed and at peace. You could see it in their faces as they tried to explain how they felt, and the words just didn't seem to exist in that moment because it's a feeling, a sense that deeply connects with the nervous system. They also noticed their symptoms would subside for a lot longer or for some they disappeared altogether after a few sessions. They would feel so much better in every sense: physically, emotionally, mentally and spiritually. Feeling like they had a lot more clarity and that they had more energy to be able to handle life situations much better than before they'd come to the sessions.

A study of sixty-two women and men participants reported significantly less tension, anger, fatigue, and depressed mood following sound meditation compared to before meditation. This study also revealed increased feelings of spiritual wellbeing, as well as faith, immediately following the sound meditation.[36]

CHAPTER 27
How Does Sound Healing Work?

Sound is vibration. 'Everything in life is vibration', as Albert Einstein once said. Sounds are all around us, every moment of every day. Scientists theorise that everything contained in the universe is in a state of vibration, from the smallest molecular structure to the largest planetary system. Some are so low that you can only feel them, rather than hear them. A considerable number of vibrations are not detectable at all.

Humans have their own vibration, their own frequency: we are basically one big-ass tuning fork. You have an innate state of being that is harmonious, where energy flows through you and around you as it should. However, when you switch into the SNS and do not come back down into a balanced, harmonised state, you begin to be pulled out of tune. No longer resonating at your natural frequency, meaning energy can no longer flow as it should, causing blockages so other systems within the body have to overcompensate in some way or another so you can still continue to function 'normally'.

When this happens again and again and again, through things like emotional traumas (big or small), stresses, physical accidents etc. then your body, mind and spirit continue to be pulled out of balance, out of tune. The ease in which you once knew to live life becomes a dis-ease, leading to a need to accommodate for these physical ailments, mental chatter and lack of joy.

Sound, like I said, is vibration and a whole combination of frequencies that can be used to aid in retuning your body back into a harmonious state. I say sound has a language of its own, just as your body does. I would even go so far as to say sound and the body have the *same* language because everything is vibration. This means our minds, the logical side of us, is the foreigner here, not understanding what is trying to be communicated to us.

Some sounds are deeply calming while others can put you on edge; some soothe and some cause resistance within the body. My belief is all are needed. Yes, it's nice to have relaxing and soothing music so your body can rest and repair but it is also extremely beneficial for the sound to cause discomfort (in the right setting, with a qualified practitioner, of course) so you can dislodge and crack through blockages and any stuck energy that has been carried in your nervous system, possibly since before your birth. Remember, you have already absorbed so much before you've even entered this world (you may want to reread the section on 'preconscious/precognitive trauma' in chapter 14). Crazy I know, but I have picked up on this imprint in sound sessions with my clients before they've told me anything about their parents' relationships – or lack thereof.

Sound healing is one of several forms of 'biofield healing'. The biofield is a large field of energy (not visible to the human eye) that surrounds each person, extending out from our body. Eileen Day McKusick compares the biofield to tree rings. The outermost edge is the gestation and birth of you, then as you make your way into the body the years go up. So, imagine your personal edge is six feet from your body, and you are sixty years old. As I move closer to you, being three feet away would represent when you were thirty years old, and being one and a half feet away from your body would symbolise you at age forty-five.

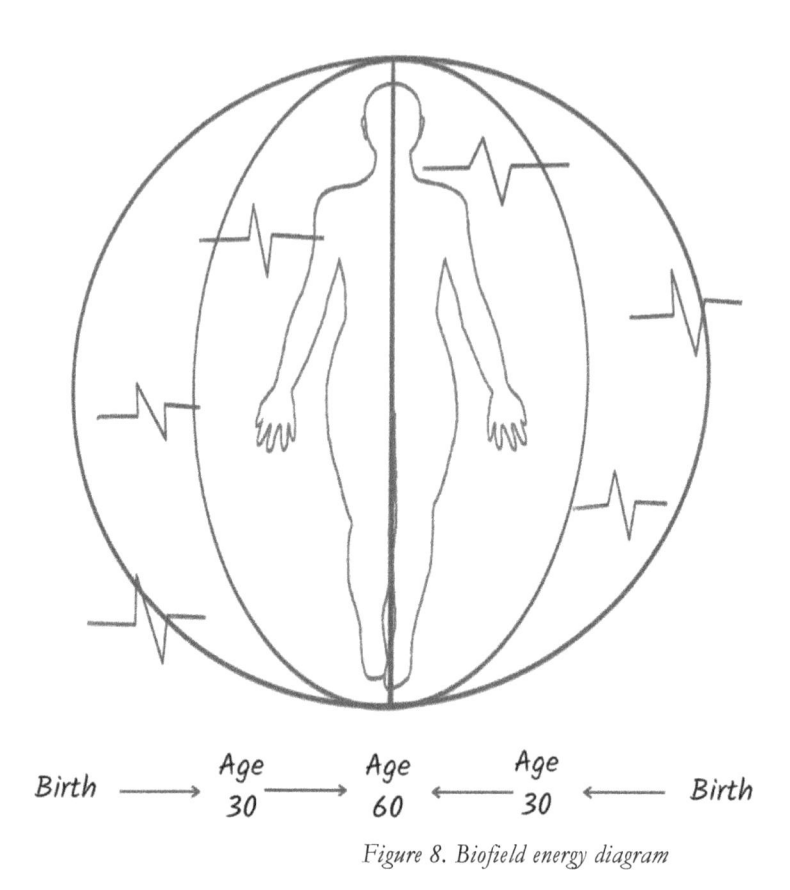

Figure 8. Biofield energy diagram

Stuck energy can be picked up by a practitioner and this tree system can help indicate when any unprocessed life experience became stored. You'd be surprised at how that energy can move just by acknowledging it and nothing else. Like I've mentioned before, awareness is key to healing.

You can even go a step further to pinpoint the possible emotion or belief that is being held in this stagnant energy. For example, practitioners who know about chakras and their seven energy centres (see below image) will know that each chakra not only has its own meaning and representation but also its own frequency and sounds so that you can chant and focus on one specific chakra.

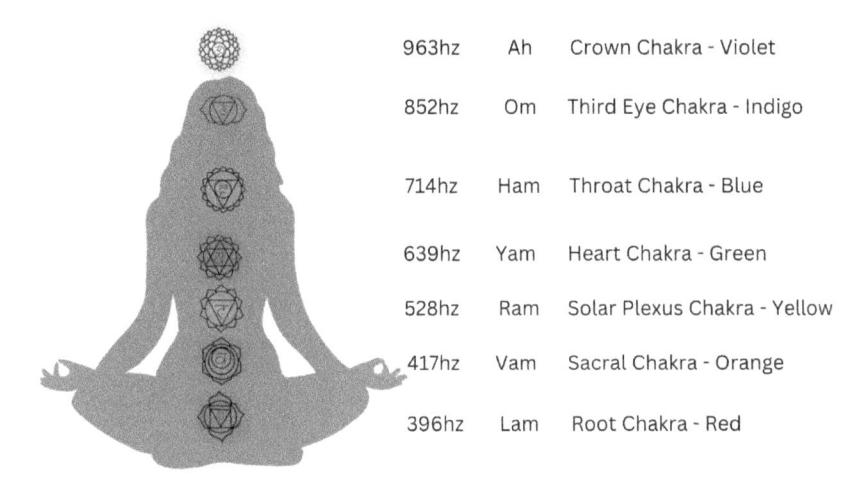

963hz	Ah	Crown Chakra - Violet
852hz	Om	Third Eye Chakra - Indigo
714hz	Ham	Throat Chakra - Blue
639hz	Yam	Heart Chakra - Green
528hz	Ram	Solar Plexus Chakra - Yellow
417hz	Vam	Sacral Chakra - Orange
396hz	Lam	Root Chakra - Red

Figure 9. The chakra system

We can take it a step further again and look at which side of the body the stuck energy is found (figure 10). Pairing the information from the chakra and the side it's connected to can help pinpoint the root cause.

RIGHT SIDE
Masculine Energy

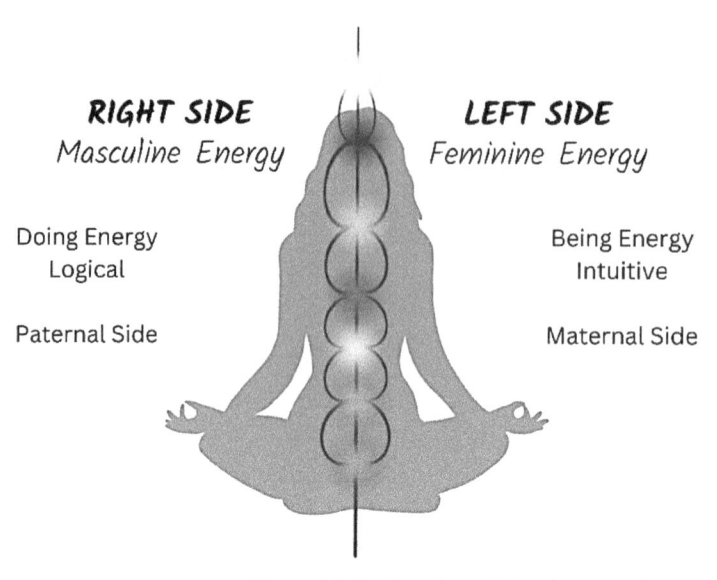

Doing Energy
Logical

Paternal Side

LEFT SIDE
Feminine Energy

Being Energy
Intuitive

Maternal Side

Figure 10. Right side and left side energy diagram

You could *even* take it a step further again, if you are aware of any issues you may have with your organs. Traditional Chinese medicine practices explain how certain emotions become stored in specific organs (figure 11). This connects massively with the vagus nerve and the PSNS.

Sadness, Depression

Lungs   Large Intestine   Skin

Fear

Kidney   Bladder

Anger, Frustration, Jealousy

Liver   Gallbladder

Worry, Anxiety, Mistrust

Stomach   Pancreas   Spleen

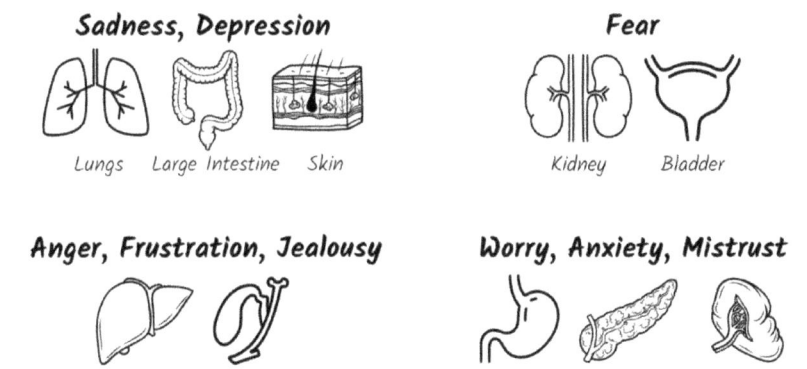

Hate, Cruelty, Impatience

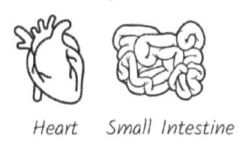

Heart   Small Intestine

Figure 11. Explanation of different organs and the feelings associated with them

Remember, too, how I mentioned about brainwaves? Well, sound is the most beautiful way to work with brainwaves and bring you down into the sweet spot of self-healing, at 7–8 Hz. Sounds help you bypass the conscious mind, the chatter and chaos of everyday living (the monkey mind if you will) and move into the unconscious. It naturally knows where to go in your body, which cells need attention, which nerves need soothing and so much more. Sound has its own intelligence. Extremely powerful shit really, if you think about it.

Your body has waves of energy traveling through and around it. Energy is meant to flow through you constantly, but if you end up storing more and more unprocessed experiences (big or small), then over time, this energy begins to build up – think of a drain clogging. Your waves of energy become distorted, meaning the natural path for energy to flow is no longer available to you. Your whole being becomes like a maze for your energy to flow. Sound healing allows vibrations to interact with the waves within and around your body. Think of the sounds as a voice, talking to someone who is agitated or sad (that's your current energy) and those sounds have the gift of the gab; the ability to brighten or calm the energy it meets. We don't need to worry about understanding this language, we can just experience it. Once they've had their chat you feel better, lighter, more focused, more optimistic, experiencing less pain or even no pain.

I had no idea that this healing would end up pairing with the next life-changing part of my journey and become a unique healing process I'd use to help clients at a deeper, more profound level of healing.

If you'd like to listen to some healing sounds, you can find them at www.hope-light.co.uk/bookresources. I highly recommend using headphones and finding a place where you won't be disturbed while listening.

CHAPTER 28

NLP

The moment my whole life changed!

In February 2019, I booked an NLP course ready for September. I prepared by listening to the hours of audio that was required before doing the course and booked my accommodation. Then in the May/June I had a flare-up of symptoms. This was somewhat normal for me, so I didn't think much about it. I ended up cancelling the course as I was panicking about how I would be able to do it since I was back in the wheelchair and feeling so shitty.

I now know that the flare-up of symptoms came about because, unconsciously, I was stressing about doing the course. Worried about the travel, staying somewhere on my own, fear that my symptoms would appear when I was there and had no one to help me. Having the flare-up of symptoms meant I wouldn't be able to do the course, therefore, I would be safe and wouldn't have to face any of the things I was worried about. My body was falling back into its autopilot to protect me from what I was anxious about. Unconsciously, of course.

The audios I had to listen to had also challenged my beliefs as I knew them. Listening to the course made me realise just how much my mind was influencing my symptoms and in turn my life. The ego mind doesn't like it when you challenge your beliefs so that, too, contributed to the flare-up.

I felt a nudge from the universe during a coaching call to rebook the course as we went into 2020. As we all know, this is when Covid-

19 decided to show up, meaning the course ended up being held online, which appeased my anxiety. It felt safe to do it.

It took away the need to travel, to be in person, and to socialize ... I hate small talk and really struggle in those types of situations. Being online meant I could stay safe in my own space and use the breaks to lie down and rest, instead of chatting. As this has been a recurring pattern when I've gone out of my comfort zone and done something on my own, the need to rest and recuperate was essential for me to 'cope'. I listened to what felt right for me and my well-being at the time. Now, however, I actually love doing in-person trainings and events because I know I won't actually die – winning – or suffer from any debilitating symptoms. Plus, when I'm doing in-person trainings and events, I am surrounded by like-minded people, and I love connecting with more awesome individuals. Especially hearing other people's stories, learning what they've overcome and how – that really gets me excited.

WHAT IS NLP, HOW DOES IT WORK?

NLP, or neuro-linguistic programming, is really fascinating when we break it down.

Neuro – This part focuses on your nervous system, the side of your mind that collects information and processes your experiences through your senses.

Linguistic – Here, we're talking about language and other ways you communicate without words. It's where you organise your thoughts and give meaning to your experiences. Basically, it's the language you use with yourself and others.

Programming – Think of this as your mental patterns or cycles. It's about recognising and using the mental programs you run to achieve your desired outcome.

I know it might sound a bit fancy, so let me break it down as simply as possible. It's basically like having an internal rule book; these rules are formed from your past experiences, and now you're living by them. But here's the kicker: these rules don't change unless you decide to change them. Nothing's set in stone. The words you speak and think shape the stories you live by; they become your reality. They can either cage you or set you free.

It might seem surprising, but neurotransmitters, usually associated with the brain, are actually present throughout the body, reaching every cell. This means you have the ability to communicate with every part of yourself. It's a gentle reminder to consider yourself as a whole, not just separate entities of mind and body. Remember earlier chapters about holistic healing and how everything is interconnected? Well, this idea fits right into that.

Consequently, the communication that you conduct in your mind, such as self-talk, thoughts of other people, as well as the spoken words you use, actually goes through your entire body. All those systems we spoke about, nervous, digestive etc. are all eavesdropping and absorbing any messages being carried to them. How, why? Because your mind does not know the difference between imagination and reality. (Another reason why meditation journeys can be so powerful).

I like to think of the mind as a computer. When you're born, it's akin to getting a new laptop – a mostly blank slate. However, even before birth, you're already absorbing information while in your mother's womb. Consider this: in utero, you're surrounded by your mother's amniotic fluid, which carries her thoughts and emotions, as we discussed in Chapter 14 on preconscious/precognitive trauma. This fluid affects the water's structure and vibration frequency around you, shaping your nervous system to adapt to hers.

Just like when you boot up a new computer and add your name, when you're born, you're given a name – your first piece of identity. It's something you didn't choose; rather, it was chosen for you based on someone else's preferences and thoughts.

Next you add software like Microsoft Office to your computer. You don't need to code anything; you just install it and trust that it will work smoothly when you click on it. Similarly, when you're born, your caregivers dress you in clothes, choosing your 'style,' until you're old enough to choose your own. The outfits you wear early on are often chosen based on their preferences and beliefs. For instance, they might think girls should wear pink, frilly dresses. As a result, you might adopt these beliefs as your own because that's all you've been exposed to. It's only when you're given the chance to explore and make choices for yourself that you can challenge and evolve your sense of identity.

Then there is a bigger programming: religious beliefs. Your parents often pass down their own beliefs, modelling and conditioning them onto you. As you grow, these beliefs shape your lived experience, becoming deeply ingrained and influencing your worldview. What your parents believe often becomes what you believe, adding another layer to your identity that you didn't actively choose for yourself.

It's not until maybe you leave home and meet people with different beliefs and life experiences that you start to question things. Sometimes you won't even question what you've grown up with because that to you is your truth. And since you've never known any different, it can be scary to make an alternative choice for many reasons, including fear of upsetting your caregivers, fear of judgment, fear of being wrong. Perhaps you have never thought about any of these things until you read this book.

CHAPTER 29

NLP In Practice

All the things I've mentioned in the previous chapter are neurological programs and internal beliefs that you hold about yourself and the world, which you can actually change if you want to. Obviously, you don't have to change a thing if you're happy with everything in your life, but I'm pretty sure you're not reading this because your life is exactly as you want it to be.

Here are the beliefs I held about myself that I uncovered on my NLP course:

- If I overdo things, I will have a flare-up in some way or another
- I have severe anxiety
- I'm poorly, I have a chronic illness
- I can't say what I think
- I'm not a very good friend
- I am a shit mum
- I'm never good enough
- I have a fear of success
- I feel guilty when I'm doing well

Write down the ones you think about yourself, especially the one you play on repeat about your illness.

The list of beliefs you've created are called 'limiting beliefs'; they are limiting stories that are played on repeat. They weave into every aspect of your life, into every cell, a story encoded into your very being, into your nervous system. Similar to a computer system, your nervous system often sticks to the same operating software until you decide it's time for an upgrade. Many of us carry on with the program passed down by our caregivers. These beliefs, experiences, and conditionings reside within us, shaping both our minds and bodies. When faced with familiar situations, your mind might gently whisper, *I remember this*, and triggers a familiar response [insert coping mechanism]. Your brain then communicates this message to the body, guiding its actions, behaviours, or reactions in that moment.

Based on your previous experiences your mind may trigger the fight-or-flight response if it senses a need for protection. It gets a bit trippy here but bear with me. Say you went somewhere on your own and you felt like everyone was staring and laughing at you. It caused you to feel embarrassed, self-conscious, rejected. Naturally, your mind seeks to shield you from such pain. So, the next time you're in a similar situation – like going out alone – it's like a mental whirlwind of worries. You fret about not finding your friends, dread the idea of interacting with strangers, fearing they might judge you. This is anxiety. Worrying about something that hasn't happened yet and trying to mentally prepare for whatever *might* happen. In its own way, your mind believes it's protecting you so you can be prepared.

Over time, this anxiety starts creeping in before the event itself. It begins as soon as you consider going somewhere alone, and in extreme cases, it becomes so overwhelming that you find it difficult to leave the house. This story plays on repeat deep within your mind, operating on autopilot without your conscious awareness. It keeps you in a perpetual state of stress, leaving you confused as to why you feel this way.

I learnt this for myself, connecting the dots between my anxiety and those pesky tremors. Once I had this knowledge and became aware that there is a deeper meaning behind what I'm experiencing, I started to take note of when the tremors would appear and what I was doing or going to do before they appeared. That's when I noticed the recurring pattern when picking up the kids, which I detailed earlier in the book (chapter 22).

What your mind doesn't understand, however, is that these protective strategies are harmful in the long run. They end up causing more distress, adding to the mum guilt, deepening the depression, and intensifying the anxiety. My mind just knew this 'protection' was effective at keeping me away from the school where I became overwhelmed. It wasn't every day, mind you; there were some days where I'd nail the school run and feel like a fucking superhero.

Most unconscious thinking happens deep within the brain, while conscious thoughts tend to occur at the surface. Like I mentioned before, your unconscious mind has been programmed by the influence of others – the media, teachers, parents, siblings etc. – and this means that others have created your reality for you and now you are running on autopilot, believing this reality is the only version of reality possible.

When you take back control, you become the creator of your own reality and this is when you can start manifesting *your* desires and not the desires of others. Yes, you are a creator and it's time you realised it. Although you created the reality you experience today, that doesn't mean you consciously chose what you are currently living in.

It means that what you were taught, conditioned into and the experiences you've lived through have created a reality based on that information.

Everything and everyone around you is a mirror of your internal world. If there is anything you don't like, change that aspect by processing the unprocessed. Covered in chapters 13 to 15 if you'd like a refresher.

Your unconscious mind's ultimate purpose is to protect you, ALWAYS! When you start to understand the mind, you will be able to make the biggest shifts in your life, opening you up to a whole new world. A world that is no longer governed by old patterns, limiting beliefs, emotions, judgements, ego.

Your ego mind will hold resistance in an attempt to protect you, but take this as a good sign: the start of you no longer living on autopilot and becoming aware of your thoughts, becoming more and more present.

How do you change your beliefs? This is where NLP techniques come in. This is when everything changed for me: when I went on a course to become a practitioner.

MY NLP PRACTITIONER EXPERIENCE

Day one of training and my whole life changed! I know that's a fucking powerful statement to make but it's also true.

By the end of the first day I was very aware of how I was labelling myself as being ill, as having M.E./CFS. It was in all my social media bios, it was how I defined myself, it was a story I was telling myself over and over again. That night I went on to all my social media and deleted anything in my bio that associated me with this old story.

I'd already booked the accommodation before the course changed to online, so I kept the booking (my mum came with me) and on the first evening my mum and I went to the sand dunes that were near where we were staying. These dunes were also a place I used to train back in the day. We walked around looking for a castle, walking up and down, dune after dune. My mum was worried I was overdoing it, but I just said, 'That's just a story, that's not actually true. It only becomes true if I allow myself to believe it.' We continued searching for what felt like hours and eventually we found it ... right by the fucking car park, hidden behind the trees. We laughed so hard. We headed back to the cottage and I was absolutely fine; no symptoms at all. This was unheard of for me, to have walked so far, up so many dunes and it was like I hadn't even been for a walk at all. My poor mind couldn't keep up with the amazement of it all.

Day two, I woke up feeling emotional. I had to lie down before training started, I felt so sick and I couldn't stop crying. On the first day, we'd been told to think about the belief we wanted to change for the next day (day two). I needed to change the belief of *If I overdo things in some way or another, I will be poorly in some way or another* – whether that was physically, emotionally, mentally or spiritually.

Training began and another person was struggling with something so the teacher, Dr Bridget, started doing some simple questioning. I followed along, focusing on the sick feeling I had and just like that, it was gone. I was amazed. It took less than a minute, I giggled to myself and thought, *Fuck yeah, I'm using that forever* and I have. I've come back to it time and time again and use it regularly with my clients for aches, pains and even emotional distress. It's called a quick change technique, which I share with you at the end of this chapter.

How is it so simple? Because we encode memories and thoughts through our five senses and language, giving meaning to every experience. Each memory has data stored to it – you can think of it as an attachment. These attachments influence the way we see the world, too. The technique above changes the data you have stored, swapping out the attachment for a new one. Essentially, changing the structure of your brain (called neuroplasticity), creating a new neural pathway to support you. You may hear it referred to as 'remapping' or 'rewiring the mind'.

Like I said before, you do not have to stay where you are, in this autopilot life and you don't have to go into the context of your experiences, your traumas. To begin shifting out of this autopilot mindset you can simply begin by practicing how to become present. Mindfulness being one of the best ways to do this, as well as breathing techniques such as the box breath on page 114 (chapter 12). You will find a super simple practice at the end of this chapter (NLP exercises).

Once you start to see your behaviours, actions, patterns and thoughts for what they are, it becomes easier to figure out why they are there. What do I mean by this? Every behaviour you have will always have a positive intention behind it. There is always a reason why you may say a certain thing, experience a certain symptom etc. It sounds silly: how can having severe stabbing pains have a positive intention?! Yet true. I share a self-enquiry technique with you at the end of the chapter so you can begin investigating your own symptoms and make a connection with the underlying positive intention that you hold.

My life-changing moment came in the form of something called a 'belief change' and it has been the most effective technique I've come across – not just for myself but also for my clients too.

We had to choose a belief we wanted to replace the old belief with: it could be anything we wanted. The very first thing that came to my mind was *I'm invincible,* so I used it because I'm awesome like that.

This belief change technique was another super simple one, just answering some questions quickly (similar to the quick change technique) about the image I saw in my head as I connected with the old limiting belief, followed by a few steps until we got to the last step, connecting with the image of me being invincible. As we moved though the last step I began crying, really crying, I could feel a change at a physiological level. There was so much happening inside me and the image in my mind was getting brighter and brighter: I felt so light, so free, so connected to the true me that had been hidden for so long. It only took about twenty to thirty minutes to do.

I think the word *powerful* is an understatement to what I experienced. I unlocked something in myself. I finally gave myself permission to believe it was possible to be well.

We had a break and I cried even harder, snots and all. They were tears of relief and joy but there was also so much grief and guilt. Grief from missing out on so much of my life and guilt for knowing that deep down, on an unconscious level, I had created the life I had been living for the past fourteen years.

That was the first day of being symptom-free. By this I mean my tremors and chronic pain disappeared, I became fully mobile and my fatigue has also gone. I occasionally get a few twitches, or get tired when I'm due on or really stressed out (as any person would) but now I am able to notice what is happening; I have an awareness and I listen to what my body is telling me. I use the tools and techniques I've learnt to help me move through it rather than becoming it.

It took between eighteen months to two years to really *believe* my symptoms were now gone. The phrase 'waiting for the other shoe to drop' comes to mind. I struggled to believe it could be so simple because everything tells us anything that effective can't be that simple and quick.

I'm not saying doing a belief change will change everyone's life but there is certainly potential that it might just do that for you. I had to take one step, followed by another, then another to open myself up to the possibility of being healed, to face things about myself, to believe in something bigger than myself. If I'd gone straight in with a belief change right after my 'destined for more moment' that I shared with you at the very start of this book, I'm not so sure it would have had such a profound effect on me. Obviously, I will never know now. Could you imagine, though, if it had all been that simple?

If you're committed to work with someone to explore and pick apart the beliefs that you have, you need to be ready to face yourself and be as raw and honest as you can with yourself. You are not consciously aware of so many things, which means it can take time to pull up those root causes, those limiting beliefs. That's one of the reasons it is easier to pick out these things in someone else than it is in yourself.

Your thoughts do not define you. They are not true, they are not reality unless you give them power.

NLP EXERCISES

The quick change technique

First, take a few breaths, setting the intention that you are releasing whatever it is that is troubling you. Now, as you ask yourself these questions, I want you to answer them as quickly as possible, like a quick-fire round on a game show.

Bring your attention to your body (I recommend closing your eyes to bring your attention into your body).

- Where in your body do you feel this?
- What shape is it?
- What colour is it?
- What texture does it have?
- What is the feeling associated with it?
- What sound do you hear?
- Pull it outside of your body: in which direction is it moving, clockwise or anticlockwise?

Now I'm going to ask you to choose different responses but still going with the very first thing that pops into your mind: no thinking, just quick-fire.

- Make it a different shape, what shape is it?
- Make it a different colour, what colour is it?
- Make it a different texture, what texture is it?
- Make it so it is spinning in a different direction, what direction is it?
- Make it so you hear a different sound, what sound do you hear?

- Make it so you have a different feeling, what feeling do you want?
- OK, amplify that feeling and place it back in your body and feel how it spreads through you.
- Great, open your eyes and notice how you feel now.

Super simple yet so effective. Head to www.hope-light.co.uk/bookresources if you'd prefer to have me asking the questions so you can just focus on answering quickly. I also recommend saying them out loud, but I totally understand it if it makes you feel silly.

Self-enquiry

Bring to mind a symptom, then use the questions below, adjusting for your own answers. I've shared my own personal example to give you an idea of how this might look for you. I'll use my own symptom of sharp stabbing pains. I had an awareness that these pains mostly came when I was at home, especially when I was trying to do things around the house.

1. What is the purpose of this symptom? What happens when you have it?

   This symptom means I have to stop what I'm doing.

2. What is the purpose of stopping what you are doing?

   To rest, and, if I'm really honest, it's so my husband and kids can see how bad I am, because saying it doesn't give me what I want or need. But screaming in pain means I'm told to rest.

3. What is it that you want and need?

Permission to rest when I need to. Currently, I only feel I can rest when I'm in pain, screaming. I'm wanting to be seen, to have attention, to be loved.

4. Do you recognise that [insert your discovery] <u>stabbing pains</u> is incongruent/contradictory with [insert your positive intention] <u>receiving love</u>?

   Yes.

5. What could you do next time this symptom appears, knowing that its positive intention is to receive love?

   I could explain what is happening to my husband and let him know the guilt I feel. I could just ask for some help in those moments instead of trying to do everything myself. I could ask just to be held for a while, to feel loved and accepted.

6. Will you give yourself permission to recognise this in the moment and ask for your positive intention instead?

   Yes.

If you have a 'No' to a yes, no question then ask yourself what is stopping you? What is the resistance? Then repeat the process of asking what is the positive intention behind this resistance. It will reveal a deeper layer to what you are experiencing.

Practicing Presence

You can do this practice anywhere. However, when starting out, I'd suggest finding a place where you can relax and take a moment to focus your attention back to yourself. It is particularly powerful when feeling anxious, stressed, or overwhelmed.

1. Take a moment to connect with your breath. Take 3 breaths. Breathing in through the nose and out through the mouth on the exhale. You can close your eyes for these breaths as a way to bring your focus to your body and the present moment.
2. Take a moment to become aware of your surroundings and name 5 things you can see e.g. TV, fireplace, trees.
3. Bring your focus back to the senses of your body and name 4 things you can feel e.g. carpet, cushion, blanket, breeze.
4. Bring your focus to your hearing and name 3 things you can hear e.g birds, children, traffic.
5. Tune into your sense of smell and name 2 things you can smell e.g. scented candle, cut grass.
6. Now tune into your sense of taste and name one thing you can taste e.g. toothpaste, coffee.
7. Take a moment to connect back with your breath and take one last breath in through your nose and out through your mouth. You can stay in this moment for as long as you need.

You can find the guided version of this practice at www.hope-light.co.uk/bookresources.

CHAPTER 30
Inner Work Yoga Teacher Training
The missing piece

After completing the NLP courses, I became fascinated by the way our minds work and craved to learn more (per my usual approach!). There was so much in my life I began to see in an entirely different light, gaining a deeper understanding of my own behaviour and triggers, and of those around me. I had so much more patience and curiosity in how my husband and kids' minds processed things, and what their internal representations were, so I could communicate with them more effectively. To learn their language.

I learnt that I communicate in details (a lot of detail!) and Lee is a big picture kind of guy. In the past, I'd let everything build up over months or even years, then lose my shit and have a three-hour breakdown with him about everything that was wrong in our relationship, and he would switch off. Never able to tell me what I was even saying to him. This then triggered me to feel ignored and rejected. I felt like I wasn't being seen or heard in my time of need. However, as a big picture person he literally could not take in all the details I was giving him, because that is not how his mind works.

Now I say in the moment when something bothers me (or sometimes just after as I need a little hissy fit first to get the annoyance out of my system). He can handle that no problem. He doesn't always take my wonderful suggestions on board but at least we can have actual conversations now.

Exploring further into self-enquiry meant there were also so many moments where I cringed or felt so stupid as I revealed the root cause behind my thoughts and triggers. At times it was really painful to face things that had become my 'normal'; things that I'd never thought about before because it was all running on autopilot at an unconscious level. Recognising how my symptoms had grown worse and worse over time because I wanted physical contact, like a hug, was beyond eye-rolling.

I think people have this delusional idea that healing is beautiful and easy, how someone will tell you how to heal but the truth is no one can do it for you, you have to be willing to dive down deep into the shadows of yourself and explore the discomfort. To meet the version of yourself that makes you cringe, makes you feel numb, makes you want to run away … and that is some scary shit.

Facing yourself is one of the hardest things you can ever do because you have to be willing to unlearn everything you currently know as truth. It is also one of the most powerful, courageous and freeing things you can do. I can't tell you how many times I have avoided facing myself. I would know something was coming up that needed to be faced and I'd push that sucker back down.

However, I learnt it always comes back around in some way or another until eventually you have no choice but to face it. There has not been one time after all these years that I regretted plunging right in and showing up for myself. Each time it was like I knew my worth and what I deserved for myself, which was freedom, relief and a deeper understanding from whatever it was that came to the surface. It has *always* outweighed any pain or sadness I may have had to feel and witness as I moved through it.

This is how I knew my journey would not stop there; there was one more stop to make. One I knew would come about at some point, from that first time I stepped on the yoga mat all those years ago. The problem I had was I didn't know what type of yoga I wanted to learn, there were just so many options that I never really researched it.

As the universe always does, it helped me out by presenting someone on Instagram I followed who had just begun her yoga teacher training. Everything she posted had me thinking, *This sounds amazing, I think this is what I've been looking for.*

I began following these teachers called Mat and Ash (their account is @theyogacouple) around 2021, but right off the bat I just didn't connect with them. It turns out their profile picture of the two of them triggered me: it felt like a perfect happy couple who were airy fairy, and all love and peace. My reaction was *No, they are too icky and lovey dovey for me.* What a judgemental bitch I was, but when you're triggered, you're triggered; what can I say, I'm human. My relationship at that time, in that moment on that day was not feeling lovey dovey. This is what I mean by your reaction to the world being a reflection of your own inner world.

I was disappointed I felt this way because the course sounded great but there was no point if I wasn't connecting with the teachers. I've done courses in the past where I didn't connect with the teacher and it became hard work to show up and in the end I didn't complete the course because, for example, their voice was just so monotonous and boring – the opposite of me.

I didn't unfollow Mat and Ash, though, and after a few months of not seeing any of their posts, one popped up. It caught my attention and I was back on their profile looking at their other posts and I didn't have the same feeling as I did last time. How you perceive and think about things can be based on where you are emotionally, physically and spiritually at that time of the event, yet on another day or after some time you're in a different place and feel very different about the same event. This is called growth.

In true Katie style I proceeded to stalk them. Suddenly everything was resonating, as if I was being called out and I loved it because I love looking deeper, at the parts of ourselves we don't like facing. I found they explained the root cause of things so perfectly, they did it in a way that was so understandable and digestible. I started to understand why I was acting certain ways and how I could work to change that. They had published a book called *The Inner Work: An Invitation to True Freedom and Lasting Happiness*, which I bought and then devoured in a few days. I was hooked and wanted to learn more. They had this perfect combination of what I had been searching for: the workings of the psyche and the deeply spiritual practices.

I love NLP, I really do, but I felt the emotional healing side hadn't been fully addressed and that is because it focuses on the messages the mind sends the body, and not at how *emotions* become stored in the body. *The Inner Work* not only explained the emotional side but broke the ego mind down so perfectly. It is now the book I recommend to all my clients so they can get to know themselves and their behaviours and actions better. To know they are not alone, that it comes down to this blueprint of limiting beliefs and the themes of consciousness that they find themselves living from. Remember that filter through which you view your life I mentioned earlier? That's what they explain so beautifully.

I really wanted to do their yoga teacher training (which included physical yoga too not just the philosophy and psychology of it), yet I still found myself umming and ahhing, unsure if they were definitely the teachers for me. I was worried I wouldn't follow through and finish it as I know I have a tendency to start something and not follow it through to the end.

As it always does, the universe provided. When Mat and Ash began advertising that they were offering a separate workshop from the training on the themes of consciousness from their book I instantly booked it. A few minutes into the first live I knew this couple were perfect for me: they were so open and honest and shared so much about their own struggles and challenges that I knew I had to do this training. Authentic through and through, I love people who aren't afraid to share the shit they've been through honestly – even if it makes them cringe – and can find the humour in it. I went on to book their year-long yoga course (and just in time too as they have now closed the school to focus on being authors).

During those twelve months of training in 2022, I went through the biggest shifts mentally, as a parent, in my business and obviously in myself. I began discovering who I was at my core, I peeled layer after layer back. I was surprised I was still being held back by so many limiting beliefs.

I discovered that I had unconsciously built my entire business to please my dad, looking for acceptance and approval from him. He had no idea I was doing it – hell, I had no idea I was doing it. I was giving my power away. I would change everything based on what he thought, without consciously being aware of what I was doing.

I became fully aware of myself doing this when I designed my second oracle deck. I was designing the box cover. I thought I had it nailed and showed my dad when he came around. I can't even remember what he said, it wasn't anything bad, just along the lines of 'I'm not sure'. My mind took that as a rejection, as not being good enough, as not pleasing him. This happened because that one moment provoked an emotion which triggered an unconscious need to protect myself from not being judged and not feeling good enough. I went on to design three more cover options because of that one seemingly insignificant conversation.

I recognised what I had done weeks, possibly months later. When I finally realised what had happened, I went back to my original design because I loved it. I finally understood that I was running on an old program that was looking to gain acceptance and love from him.

The inner work yoga training brought up so many triggering moments and it was such a challenge at times to continue studying because there were so many 'aha!' moments, but such moments often involved having to come face to face with a part of myself that had been living in the darkness; the shadows of myself. I would have to pause and take the time I needed to process before moving on to the next module.

This can be known as a healing crisis: where things seem to be falling apart after recognising something, acknowledging a part of yourself – you can even dip into depression or get flu-like symptoms.

I've even ended up throwing up a few hours after a sound healing session. It was a cleansing – albeit a fucking deep energy cleansing – but it was all about energy moving and shifting at a cellular level. I just had to trust the process and ride the wave.

I can hand on heart say I have become a much better mum since doing this training, which is not something I expected to happen at all. It has been such a humbling journey and I cannot tell you how many times I've repeated *I did the best I could with the resources I had at the time* to myself. It's a mantra I say to myself when I find I'm beating myself up for the past or for all the things I didn't do as a mum, the things I never said, the things I created in myself because my needs weren't being met.

When you realise just how much of you now comes from your childhood you become hyperaware of yourself as a parent. My first thoughts were, *Well, Isabelle's anxiety has clearly been taught to her by me even before she was born and Matthew's people-pleasing was conditioned into him from when I was poorly and he began looking after me at the age of three.*

I actually began writing this book the day after an inner work call with Mat. It was the first time I really told someone my story, from start to finish and I was so open and honest throughout the call. I began physically shaking while telling my story. I was shocked and there was a small part of me that thought *fuck, what have I done! What if I just triggered the tremors to start again?* Then I reminded myself that shaking is one of the body's ways to release trauma, to allow the stress cycle to finally complete. Just like when a lion chases a gazelle. The gazelle goes in to flight mode but once the threat has passed (provided it didn't get caught of course) it has a good shake and then continues about its day like it was no big deal.

So instead of fighting the shaking – like I would have in the past. I embraced it, allowed it and let Mat know what was going on. He allowed me to just experience it, to feel it. After a few minutes the shaking began to ease until eventually it all stopped. The healing I experienced in this call left me with this sense of permission to finally write my story.

Awareness is key to learning what your body is experiencing and what its needs are.

I realised I'd grown up living in a space of judgement; it was the filter through which I saw the world. So when the affair came out, I came from that same place and I attached to it all. This was followed by living in a place of hopelessness for many years, so attached to the belief that this is it for me. I eventually stepped into grief, letting go of the old version of who I had been so I could open myself up to the possibility of a new, better version of myself. I had to relearn how to live. Something so simple to many but to me, it was foreign.

This led to two years of being stuck in fear not long after starting my healing business in 2018. A fear of who I would be without an illness, what I would do, but also fear of the financial implications as I would no longer be on benefits but unsure I'd be well enough to work, to really earn money without any payback of fatigue, which in turn created fatigue – a form of protection. This kept me safe, kept me in what I knew and took the stress of 'what ifs' away because with a flare up I didn't have to try, I didn't have to make any decisions that may lead me to being wrong and causing the symptoms to worsen.

After acknowledging that fear was holding me back from really living life I finally stepped into desire. A need and want for something more. A place to dream of all possibilities, like writing a book and working part-time with people who need support, just as I had.

This inner work yoga teacher training was so much more than yoga training: it was an unlearning of life, an awakening, an upleveling and a realisation that every single person is whole, innocent and unconditionally loved at all times, no matter what they've been through or done.

If you have no awareness of the ego your ego will lead the way, creating layer upon layer of false beliefs – based on unprocessed life experiences – warping your realities since childhood. The ego is a program, a thought process, a perspective. It is essentially an illusion, an accumulation of thoughts, feelings and beliefs that have now turned itself into a *me* identity.

Nonetheless, the ego is not an enemy, it is not a bad thing, it gives life meaning and purpose; it makes life that much richer. The ego's greatest fear is death, which can manifest in many ways such as gaining status, money, beauty, knowledge, immortality. It makes time more cherished.

Suffering, however, only starts when you begin to identify yourself as the experience, creating that illusion, losing yourself in it, taking things too seriously, stunting the natural flow of energy. When experiencing pain, suffering, discomfort, experiences that are negative or perceived as negative, the ego will resist, leading to suffering as it attaches to these experiences when in fact, they are lies. They were just an experience that passed, end of. It is only you who attaches meaning to it.

You can find both physical yoga and inner work videos to follow at www.hope-light.co.uk/bookresources.

CHAPTER 31
The Themes Of Consciousness

When I began learning about the themes of consciousness, I became fascinated by how everything seemed to fall into these categories. I was introduced to these themes through *The Inner Work* – the book I mentioned in the last chapter. Reading this book was like an awakening, my mind seeing so much in a different light. I gained a deeper understanding of myself and where my behaviours came from.

When I did their workshop on the themes of consciousness, where they delved even deeper into the themes, I was blown away. I could recognise myself in so many different ways. Like how a chronic illness is very much the theme of overwhelm, which is when you experience hopelessness. You find your thoughts go along the lines of *What's the point, why bother? It's too much, I can't, I'm a burden, nothing will work.* Sound familiar?

When you can recognise which theme is most prevalent for you, you can begin to learn what will help move you out of this theme and into one that is more supportive. It doesn't mean you instantly go from this overwhelming feeling of being a burden to being enlightened. It's a process. You just focus on where you are now, and take the next baby step. For overwhelm, it's about asking for help and being willing to face the heavy emotions of grief and loss. The loss of identity to grieve the person you remember yourself being before becoming ill. That was one of the hardest things I had to do because I would have to finally let go of the previous version of myself. The one I held on a pedestal.

Once I got to this point, I found myself in a place of fear. If I let go of who I was, then who is left? That was terrifying to me. My mind was telling me that I was giving up hope. Hope of being whole again. Why was it doing this? Because the ego mind becomes triggered about the unknown. Remember, your ego works purely on past experiences. Letting go of the past you means it doesn't know what will come next, which means the ego doesn't know if it exists there, which means it has to do all it can to keep you where you are because it believes you are safe in what you know.

Yet, the truth is, that old version of me stopped existing the moment I became ill. I have been through so many experiences and challenges since then. I have grown up, got married, had kids. I have learnt how strong I am and what I can overcome. If I went back to the old version of who I was, I wouldn't have any of the skills I have now and dare I say the wisdom too. I wouldn't be able to face discomfort and obstacles that life throws my way. I now face such obstacles in a healthy way that doesn't have a long-term impact on my mind, body and spirit.

There are many theories about the themes of consciousness. What follows is my understanding from the eight themes of consciousness explored in *The Inner Work*. Each theme comes back to the limiting themes where the ego is always contradicting itself, meaning the ego will tell you one thing but in reality, you get something else.

1. **Shame & Rejection**

Ego – You're unlovable so I'm going to reject you first before the world can reject you.

Reality – You push everyone out of your life, telling everyone you're unlovable so you never get rejected. And you end up rejected anyway.

2. **Guilt & Judgement**

Ego – If you blame everyone else for your condition then you'll never have to face your condition.

Reality – You keep yourself in it because you blame everyone else instead of doing something about it.

Ego – To avoid being judged I'm going to keep you safe by judging you first.

Reality – You're filled with self-doubt and self-criticism.

3. **Hopelessness**

Ego – I'm trying to help you not get heartbroken or disappointed.

Reality – You feel everything is hopeless and there's no point in even trying.

4. **Grief & Regret**

Ego – If you hold on really tight, you'll avoid losing.

Reality – You experience loss greatly as you never thought you would lose it.

5. **Fear**

Ego – I'm going to protect you, keep you safe, e.g. don't go out or you will end up exhausted.

Reality – You're bound in a prepared state of panic, fear and even isolated.

6. **Desire**

Ego – You need to get this thing so you can feel loved and wanted.

Reality – You feel less wanted and loved because you realise it didn't actually fulfil anything. It gave you a temporary high, leading you to crave something bigger.

7.   **Anger**

Ego – You need to get everyone out of your way and eliminate any obstacle or enemies, then you won't have any enemies.

Reality – You create new enemies.

8.   **Pride**

Ego – Do this and everyone will respect you, e.g. jump off a building into a pool.

Reality – You get the opposite reaction and people think less highly of you, e.g. 'What an idiot'.

Shame is the most common theme for many people – not just those with a chronic illness. I will share some examples around this:

Adultery lives in the theme of shame. Shame comes from a place of believing you are unlovable and will always be rejected. You may have thoughts like *I'm worthless, I'm disgusting, I'm unforgivable, I can't be loved.* When you believe yourself to be these things – to be unlovable – your actions and behaviours, such as an affair, proves just how unlovable you are: rejecting yourself of worthiness, of love, ultimately leading to losing what you did have. In the end proving the ego right because everyone left, leaving you perceiving yourself to be unlovable all along. A self-fulfilling prophecy.

My husband and I had this exact same wound: he said nobody wants him, which broke my heart. I reminded him that he is wanted and he should know me well enough by now to know I wouldn't stick around if I believed otherwise.

I began putting two and two together, recognising that his behaviour and actions in our marriage of not showing up for the kids or for me at times were his ego's way of protecting himself. Pushing us away in many different ways, blaming me or the kids for things, instead of owning it himself; the narcissistic side of shame. We all have it in us, including me, so don't think I'm trying to paint a bad picture of him. I was just like him when we first met and for *years* after, until I started putting in the work.

For me, I believed I'd never have a long-lasting relationship. I avoided them as a teenager, that's why my first boyfriend was Lee, when I was eighteen. And I only agreed because he was so persistent. I thought it wouldn't last long as I was poorly and no one would stick around for what I was experiencing, plus all the anger and frustration that came with it. He proved me so very wrong. Not that it helped: I still believed unconsciously he'd leave so I'd slam cupboard doors in annoyance when he pissed me off, I'd not speak to him for three days when I was angry with him (and I mean not a word: maybe a grunt here and there, but that was it).

There have been two specific times when I've felt completely done with our marriage. When I thought *This is it, he'll leave now. This is a perfect out for him.* As if I was doing him a favour. Don't get me wrong, there were actual issues and reasons why I felt what I felt, but it stems from a feeling of not being lovable, exacerbated by the fact that neither of us could talk about our emotions to be able to communicate in a healthy way. It always ended up in arguments, with nothing being resolved. I didn't fully understand where this limiting belief came from until I was finishing writing this very book! I share what I learnt about this particular root cause in the following chapter.

While learning about the themes of consciousness, I realised that Lee's ego is constantly trying to prove that he is unwanted, unlovable so I will finally reject him as he always believed I would, unconsciously. Then he'd be able to say *See, I told you no one wants me*. Yet, I am still here, plodding along as I try and share the knowledge and understanding that I have, so he can finally see how madly and hopelessly in love I am with him and that he is truly wanted.

Unfortunately, the thing about healing is no one can do it for you, no matter how much they love you. It is something you have to face and recognise for yourself. Don't misunderstand me, he is much better at listening and working with me now than he ever has been before, I just know that belief still lingers deep down and he still has more work to do.

I, on the other hand, have been putting in the work, learning to voice my emotions, to say when something hurts my feelings, but the biggest shift came this year (2023) when I finally let him all the way in (only took me fourteen years!). At last, I told Lee how dark my mind got and the thoughts I had. Since then, I've been facing a new feeling of insecurity: now he knows all of it, he will be done with me. That I'm too much, too broken for him. It's the part I'd been hiding from because that is the root of it all. That feeling of being unlovable. It's like the last layer has been peeled back and now I have to manoeuvre through these new, raw emotions to truly begin healing this deep wound that everyone will leave if they see my real thoughts in the dark moments.

Why do I share all this? Because I want you to know you are not alone in your own experiences, that what you uncover about yourself is not necessarily unique, that you won't be the only one to have certain thoughts or feelings about yourself, as we all want to be loved and accepted at the core of it all.

You are *so much* more than your thoughts and you are *not* defined by your past: it is not your true identity. When you begin stripping away these layers, you start seeing them for what they are … those *lies*! You finally begin to see the real truth underneath it all, seeing the light in the dark, the path forward towards your Hope-Light.

CHAPTER 32
What Has All This Taught Me?
Acceptance

When I began this journey nearly a decade ago, back in 2015, when I listened to the voice telling me I was destined for so much more, I didn't know that would be the start of my healing journey. I still had a lot of hurt and pain that I held towards my dad even though by that stage I saw him regularly, had a laugh with him and even lived with him for a few months.

This journey has given me such a gift: not just getting my life back, but being able to see my dad for who he really is ... human. An imperfect human, just as we all are. A person who has been through his own shit, who has had his own traumas and done the best he could with the resources he had at the time.

You can't tell me you've never made mistakes. I know I have. Even writing this book, I fucked up and hurt my dad because I didn't go the right way about talking to him about what I put in the book. I felt terrible after the conversation. I was physically shaking while on the phone – trauma response – then I cried so hard after the call, telling myself *I'm so stupid*. I let myself embrace all that was coming up, not trying to fight it but to just let it be, to acknowledge what was arising. Then I sat with myself and asked myself a few questions, so I thought I'd share them with you.
1. Am I really stupid?

No, I fucked up and I held my hands up to that. I've taken responsibility for my actions. I understand how I hurt him and I apologised.

2. Why did I leave it all so long to talk to him about it?
   Because I was scared
3. What was I scared of?
   I was scared of his reaction, scared he will tell me I'm wrong. I was also scared that it would hurt him and/or trigger him due to the parts about myself that he doesn't know about. I was scared he would think less of me and I was scared he would make me feel like I was not good enough and feel rejected.
4. How can I move forward from this point?
   Firstly, I can allow myself to feel proud that I am at a point where I can recognise my mistakes instead of becoming reactive to them. Secondly, remind myself that there is nothing I can do to change it now, holding on to the guilt won't do anything for anyone. It literally does nothing other than make me feel shitty about myself and my internal berating won't make him feel better. Thirdly, acknowledge that carrying the guilt would mean I'm attaching to it and in turn causing a dis-ease within my body. Lastly, know that I can strive to do better in the future. I can't change the past but I can choose to deal with things differently moving forward.

  What you feel is what you feel and sometimes, until you're called out on your behaviour, you don't always know what you're doing until you or someone else brings an awareness to it.

  The knowledge I have gained has allowed me to not only understand myself but to understand those around me, including my dad. Understanding he has his own traumas from childhood, then he had PTSD from his time in the army that played out in my childhood. Understanding he has his own limiting beliefs programmed into him, too. Like I said, just like any other human being.

I have finally accepted myself more than I have ever been able to accept myself; no longer looking for acceptance from outside of myself. As I now know I am enough as I am and that there is no such thing as broken, just wounded; just patterns and programmes written long ago that can be changed at any time with a little bit of love, courage and conviction.

Writing this book has been such an up and down journey. There have been many things that came back to me that I'd forgotten. As I've opened up to my mum about things I've written or realised, I've learnt things about her and what she experienced. This year, 2023, was one of the hardest years with my mental health but I continue to work on myself and face it with the tools and techniques I've learnt and getting help so I don't face anything alone anymore.

I have found the whole process of writing this book cathartic and healing – so much so that I considered not publishing it. It just all felt so insignificant; like it was no longer relevant because I'd already healed so many emotions along the way. I have detached from so much of what I was taking on as my identity and I have recognised more limiting beliefs as I've worked through this process.

However, the biggest discovery I have made is that as much as I thought my illness was caused by the fallout from the affair, it actually traces back further to a much younger age. The initial unprocessed life experience occurred when I was around five-years-old and had hand, foot, and mouth disease. I refused to eat; my dad was away, and they had to call him back home. He came home, and when he tried to feed me, I'd eat for him.

You see, I was a massive daddy's girl. I adored him, but when he went away, five-year-old me felt abandoned, rejected, and unloved. I was hurting and sad. It's a natural feeling to have at that age as you are still so dependent on your caregivers for love and safety.

So when I was poorly and he came back, my mind and body remembered that association: be poorly and love and security return. That association was stored in my unconscious as a 'program' ready to run anytime those feelings of insecurity and abandonment reared their ugly heads again.

Fast-forward to teenage Katie, when my dad left again, but this time more permanently. That dormant, unprocessed experience from my childhood was triggered, resurrecting the same feelings, emotions, and beliefs my five-year-old self experienced. My mind and body recalled that the last time I felt like this, I just wanted my daddy, and when I got sick he returned. So, the symptoms worsened and became more aggressive. Unconsciously, my mind and body believed that if I became ill enough, he would have to come back, and I would be safe again – that was the belief I unconsciously clung to, because it was the belief of five-year-old me.

By that point, however, another part of me would have hated it if he had come back, because of the new, unprocessed life experiences and raw emotions now attached to him, all layered on top of the initial trauma, plus the layers I had accumulated since being five-years-old. That's a lot of unprocessed shit for my poor juvenile mind to deal with, right? These new wounds embedded the belief that I was not wanted. It was much deeper at this point, hence the battle with a much more severe 'invisible illness'.

So, yeah, it was a fascinating revelation after all these years. Who would have thought that after being so fixated and certain that the root cause was definitely due to one specific event, it would, in fact, be connected to multiple layers that were already 'alive' in my nervous system, just waiting to be reignited once again? Only this time, with more and more wounds added, fuelling the fire of the original limiting belief that I'm not wanted and will always be abandoned.

CHAPTER 33
What I Hope For You

I hope this book has opened you up to new possibilities, new healing opportunities and many, many realisations to finally be able to see yourself for the true version of you underneath the lies, the layers of life experiences and more.

I hope you understand that just reading a book will not heal you, that you have to be willing to put in the work, even if it means feeling things you don't want to. Give yourself time and have patience with yourself and where you are now. There is no quick fix, but take comfort knowing it can happen much quicker than what I experienced, because unlike me, you are starting with the knowledge, resources and understanding of the connection and anatomy of the mind, body and spirit.

For me, I couldn't (or wouldn't) allow myself to visualise myself as being healed and I hope this book has given you permission to visualise that for yourself.

Remember, there is nothing 'wrong' with you; you are whole. It is just unhealed wounds, outdated coping mechanisms and a need to survive. Remember, too, that you are alive even after everything you've experienced. Trust that you will continue that way even if you take a step into the unknown.

I send you all my love and support for the journey that is about to unfold in front of you. Start today by asking yourself, *What do I want to work on today?* Then use the questions on the following page to dig a little deeper into what might be causing this. You will likely find the cause is unrelated to what you assume it to be. I invite you to be honest and open with yourself. In fact, be brutally honest. In this work, there are no judgements, just awareness and the option to choose something different.

EMOTIONAL ENQUIRY EXERCISE

Remember, this is not about forcing anything but simply bringing awareness to the mind, body and spirit. Do not doubt what you feel or anything that arises. Your unconscious knows what you need: all you have to do is trust the first thing that arises. This is a practice; it can take time to trust your intuition, that knowing that you always have. The more you do this, the easier it gets.

- What do I want to address today? Name the feeling, the emotion associated with it. (Use the wheel of emotion chart on page 149 if you're struggling to name it).
- Where are you physically feeling it in your body?
- What is this emotion bringing up?
- What is the first memory that comes to mind as you connect and sit with this emotion?
- When was the first time you experienced this emotion?
- What belief do you hold here?
- What do you need to learn from this experience so you can release this emotion today?

MY HOPES

I hope that this book has brought you towards healing in some way. I hope that if you have found it useful in any way at all that you would want to share it with others. I hope to touch the lives of many. To let as many people as I can know that where they currently are is not where they have to stay. There is so much more out there if you are willing to look past the fear, past the unknown and surrender to the what ifs: *What if I am well? What if I can do all that I dream of? What if I become better than I ever dreamed possible? What if I see myself as whole?*

I hope for a better world, as I'm sure you do too. One where my children understand that they are not their experiences, that they have choice and a voice. I hope the next generation look at each other and say *I see you, I see your past pain, I understand that this action, this behaviour is not who you truly are. I understand that; I understand you. I understand that there is hope and light that lies within you and I will hold your hand as you learn how to set it free from within yourself.*

My biggest hope of all is that you too now feel the compassion you've been lacking for yourself, to know where you are is not the end and that you too are destined for more. I hope you have been able to open yourself up to the belief that there are more possibilities that lie before you than you first believed when you started this book. All you need to do is to take that first step, and from there you take it one step at a time. Be kind and gentle with yourself but most of all don't give up! There is a light within you, no matter how small or dim it may seem right now. You can nurture that light, coax it to burn brighter, to become stronger and eventually set fire to that feeling of hope once more. It is my belief that hope never truly dies, there is always a spark, it just might need the right resources, the right encouragement and at times a bucket full of patience before you can feel the full force run through you.

Remember, your journey won't be the same as mine. You don't have to do the things I did; just be open to exploring alternatives that work for you. Maybe NLP sounded good to you, but other things didn't resonate. That's OK. Just keep your eyes open. The universe will show you what you need – just be ready to receive it and take the brave steps toward your own healing journey, whatever that looks like for you. Now go and be fucking awesome!

Recommended Reading

The Inner Work *by Mathew Micheletti and Ashley Cottrell*

Girl Code *by Cara Alwill Leyba*

You are a Badass *by Jen Sincero*

The Universe Has Your Back *by Gabrielle Bernstein*

She Means Business *by Carrie Green*

#Girlboss *by Sophia Amoruso*

Tuning the Human Biofield *by Eileen Day McKusick*

Electric Body, Electric Health *by Eileen Day McKusick*

The Breathing Cure *by Patrick McKeown*

You Can Heal Your Life *by Louise Hay*

The Hidden Messages in Water *by Masaru Emoto*

Reiki Made Easy *by Torsten A. Lange*

Diagnosis and Treatment of Chronic Fatigue Syndrome *by Sarah Myhill*

The Fast Way to Slow Down Ageing *by Sheri Dixon*

Acknowledgements

There have been so many people that have helped me on my journey of awesomeness. I want to take a moment to name a few people who have made an everlasting impression in my life.

Obviously, I will have to start with my husband, **Lee Roy**. The poor guy has endured all the highs and lows of this journey with me, and let me tell you, there have been more twists and turns than a roller coaster ride! But hey, he's still standing, and so am I, so I reckon we're doing something right! He has been the hero and the villain in my story, just as I have been to him. I am so grateful to have found someone who matches my awesome.

Isabelle and Matthew, my trusty sidekicks, never failing to lift my spirits and boost my confidence when doubt started creeping in. They've been my saving grace, whether it's lending a hand on those hard days or joining me in making fun of the chaos that was our lives.

My **Mum**, an absolute legend in her own right. She's gone above and beyond, not just for me, but for Lee and the kids too. Words can't express the depth of gratitude I feel for her - though she'd probably say, 'Aw, shucks, it's all in a day's work!'. She showered me with endless love, celebrating all the highs with me and holding my hand through the darkness.

My **Dad**, even though our relationship has been an emotional rollercoaster at times, despite the challenges we've faced I've come to recognise the essence of who you truly are. I do not hold the anger and hurt I once did. I can finally see you. I also believe that what we've been through has allowed me to discover and develop my own strength, mentally, physically and emotionally.

Salli aka 'The Wifey', thank you for being you. You have been there through all the ups and downs. Whether it's through tears from the anger and hatred I held towards my body or as my very own source of entertainment with your dark humour, pure awesomeness and horse face.

Kayleigh Phillips and Sara Dobler, thank you for being there for me during my teenage years while I was attempting to deal with so many emotions. You both brought me joy and laughter during those challenging times. Staying with you or training together always gave me something to look forward to. When I was with you, I could finally get out of my own head, and everything felt a little bit easier.

Ffion Haf Davies, thank you for putting up with all my shit as a teenager, especially my bitchy, judgmental self. It couldn't have been easy for you but know I will be eternally grateful for you. You were always there for me, even when I pushed you away. You were a calm within the storm on many occasions. And, of course, a big thank you to your Mum and Dad, **Jackie and Hefin Davies**, for opening your home to me, creating a sanctuary where I always felt safe.

Kimberley Walker, Robyn Eadon, Catherine Evans & Jade Jones, you took the time out of your days to visit my miserable arse, and I am so grateful. If you guys hadn't popped in, I would have gone months and months without seeing anyone other than my family. You were a joyous spark in my dark days, a reason to get up and maybe even wash my hair.

Sian Smith, the most amazing editor. This book would not be the same without you and all your awesome word suggestions, sentence structure, layout – the list really does go on. Thank you so much for all your support and feedback, and of course, thank you for embracing my swearing.

Raven Crest Books, a huge thank you for helping this book reach more eyes. Without you, it might have been lost in the digital abyss, where memes roam free and cat videos reign supreme. Thank you for helping me to share my voice with those struggling to survive the chronic illness life.

ARC readers, I cannot thank you enough for giving your time to read this book, picking up spelling mistakes, and sharing your favourite parts with me. You have made the process of publishing a lot less stressful and have also improved the quality of this book, so thank you very much.

How to Work with Me

Katie Rose Jones
Owner of Hope-Light
Trauma-Informed Holistic Therapist

Instagram: @HopeLightUK
Facebook: @HopeLightUK
YouTube: @HopeLightUK
Website: hope-light.co.uk
Email: info@hope-light.co.uk

Katie lives in the beautiful countryside of West Wales, UK, and works with clients both in person and online. She offers free connection calls, so if you'd like to have a chat and see if her work is for you, just reach out!

References

1 Bernell S, Howard SW, 'Use Your Words Carefully: What Is a Chronic Disease?', *Front Public Health*, 4 (2016), doi: https://doi.org/10.3389/fpubh.2016.00159
2 https://www.nice.org.uk/guidance/ng206/chapter/Context
[3] https://www.nice.org.uk/guidance/ng206/chapter/Context
[4] https://www.cdc.gov/me-cfs/about/
[5] Falk Hvidberg M, Brinth LS, Olesen AV, Petersen KD, Ehlers L, 'The Health-Related Quality of Life for Patients with Myalgic Encephalomyelitis / Chronic Fatigue Syndrome (ME/CFS), *PLoS One*, 6 (2015), Jul doi: https://doi.org/10.1371/journal.pone.0132421
[6] https://www.waterstones.com/book/how-to-live-when-you-could-be-dead/deborah-james/9781785043604
[7] McCorry LK, 'Physiology of the Autonomic Nervous System', *Am J Pharm Educ*. 71(4) (2007), 78, https://www.ncbi.nlm.nih.gov/pmc/articles/PMC1959222/
[8] Corrigan Frank, Fisher J, Nutt David, 'Autonomic Dysregulation and the Window of Tolerance Model of the Effects of Complex Emotional Trauma', *Journal of Psychopharmacology*, 25 (2011), 17-25. https://journals.sagepub.com/doi/10.1177/0269881109354930
[9] Breit S, Kupferberg A, Rogler G, Hasler G, 'Vagus Nerve as Modulator of the Brain-Gut Axis in Psychiatric and Inflammatory Disorders', *Front Psychiatry*, 9:44 (2018). https://www.ncbi.nlm.nih.gov/pmc/articles/PMC5859128/
[10] Lewis SJ, Arseneault L, Caspi A, Fisher HL, Matthews T, Moffitt TE, Odgers CL, Stahl D, Teng JY, Danese A, 'The epidemiology of trauma and post-traumatic stress disorder in a representative cohort of young people in England and Wales', *Lancet Psychiatry*. 6(3), (2019), 247-256. https://www.ncbi.nlm.nih.gov/pmc/articles/PMC6384243/
[11] https://www.kingsfund.org.uk/projects/time-think-differently/trends-disease-and-disability-long-term-conditions-multi-morbidity
[12] NIHR, 'Multiple long-term conditions (multimorbidity): making sense of the evidence' (March 2021), https://evidence.nihr.ac.uk/collection/making-sense-of-the-evidence-multiple-long-term-conditions-multimorbidity/
[13] Davis EP, Sandman CA. The timing of prenatal exposure to maternal cortisol and psychosocial stress is associated with human infant cognitive development. Child Dev. 2010 Jan-Feb;81(1):131-48. doi: 10.1111/j.1467-8624.2009.01385.x. PMID: 20331658; PMCID: PMC2846100.

[14] Crawley E, Davey Smith G, 'Is chronic fatigue syndrome (CFS/ME) heritable in children, and if so, why does it matter?', *Arch Dis Child*, 92(12), (2007), 1058–61. https://www.ncbi.nlm.nih.gov/pmc/articles/PMC2066085/
[15] https://www.cdc.gov/genomics/disease/epigenetics.htm
[16] Dias B, Ressler K, 'Parental olfactory experience influences behavior and neural structure in subsequent generations', *Nat Neurosci* 17, (2014), 89–96. https://pubmed.ncbi.nlm.nih.gov/24292232/
[17] Willcox, G. (1982). The Feeling Wheel: A Tool for Expanding Awareness of Emotions and Increasing Spontaneity and Intimacy. *Transactional Analysis Journal*, 12(4), 274-276. https://doi.org/10.1177/036215378201200411
[18] Bergsma, A, 'Do self-help books help?', *Journal of Happiness Studies* 9 (2008), 341–360. https://doi.org/10.1007/s10902-006-9041-2
[19] Den Boer P, Wiersma D, Van Den Bosch R, (2004). 'Why is self-help neglected in the treatment of emotional disorders? A meta-analysis', *Psychological Medicine*, 34(6), (2004), 959-971. https://pubmed.ncbi.nlm.nih.gov/15554567/
[20] http://www.gostress.com/stress-facts
[21] https://www.apa.org/topics/mindfulness/meditation
[22] Bashir M, Bhagra A, Kapa S, & McLeod C, 'Modulation of the autonomic nervous system through mind and body practices as a treatment for atrial fibrillation', *Reviews In Cardiovascular Medicine*, 20(3) (2019), 129. https://doi.org/10.31083/j.rcm.2019.0
[23] Tomczyk J, Nezlek JB, & Krejtz I, 'Gratitude Can Help Women At-Risk for Depression Accept Their Depressive Symptoms, Which Leads to Improved Mental Health', *Front Psychology*, 13 (2022), https://www.ncbi.nlm.nih.gov/pmc/articles/PMC9022718/
[24] Braun TD, Uebelacker LA, Ward M, Holzhauer CG, McCallister K, & Abrantes A, '"We really need this": Trauma-informed yoga for Veteran women with a history of military sexual trauma', *Complementary Therapies in Medicine*, 59 (2021), https://www.sciencedirect.com/science/article/pii/S0965229921000704?via %3Dihub
[25] Oka T, Tanahashi T, Chijiwa T, Lkhagvasuren B, Sudo N & Oka K, 'Isometric yoga improves the fatigue and pain of patients with chronic fatigue syndrome who are resistant to conventional therapy: a randomized, controlled trial', *Biopsychosocial Medicine* 14 (2014), https://www.ncbi.nlm.nih.gov/pmc/articles/PMC4269854/pdf/13030_2014_ Article_27.pdf
[26] Oka T, Tanahashi T, Sudo N. et al., 'Changes in fatigue, autonomic functions, and blood biomarkers due to sitting isometric yoga in patients with chronic fatigue syndrome' *Biopsychosocial Medicine* 12 (2018), https://doi.org/10.1186/s13030-018-0123-2

[27] Jerath R, Edry JW, Barnes VA & Jerath V, 'Physiology of long pranayamic breathing: neural respiratory elements may provide a mechanism that explains how slow deep breathing shifts the autonomic nervous system', *Medical Hypotheses* 67(3) (2006), 566–71, https://pubmed.ncbi.nlm.nih.gov/16624497/
[28] Cheng KS, Croarkin PE & Lee PF, 'Heart Rate Variability of Various Video-Aided Mindful Deep Breathing Durations and Its Impact on Depression, Anxiety, and Stress Symptom Severity', *Mindfulness*, 10 (2019), 2082–2094, DOI: 10.1007/s12671-019-01178-8
[29] Jerath R, Edry JW, Barnes VA & Jerath V, 'Physiology of long pranayamic breathing: neural respiratory elements may provide a mechanism that explains how slow deep breathing shifts the autonomic nervous system', *Medical Hypotheses* 67(3) (2006), 566–71, https://pubmed.ncbi.nlm.nih.gov/16624497/
[30] Tang Y, Ma Y, Fan Y, Feng H, Wang J & Feng S. et al. (2009). 'Central and autonomic nervous system interaction is altered by short-term meditation', *Proceedings Of The National Academy Of Sciences*, 106(22) (2009), 8865-8870, https://pubmed.ncbi.nlm.nih.gov/19451642/
[31] Bashir M, Bhagra A, Kapa S, & McLeod C, (2019). 'Modulation of the autonomic nervous system through mind and body practices as a treatment for atrial fibrillation', *Reviews In Cardiovascular Medicine*, 20(3) (2019), 129, https://pubmed.ncbi.nlm.nih.gov/31601087/
[32] Lutz A, Greischar LL, Rawlings NB, Ricard M & Davidson RJ, 'Long-term meditators self-induce high-amplitude gamma synchrony during mental practice', *PNAS*, 101 (46) (2004), https://doi.org/10.1073/pnas.0407401101
[33] Tomas C, Brown A, Strassheim V, Elson JL, Newton J & Manning P, 'Cellular bioenergetics is impaired in patients with chronic fatigue syndrome', *PLoS One*, 12 (10) (2017), https://www.ncbi.nlm.nih.gov/pmc/articles/PMC5655451/
[34] Dyer NL, Baldwin AL & Rand WL, 'A Large-Scale Effectiveness Trial of Reiki for Physical and Psychological Health', *Journal of Alternative and Complementary Medicine*, 12 (2019), https://pubmed.ncbi.nlm.nih.gov/31638407/
35 Baldwin AL, Vitale A, Brownell E, Kryak E & Rand W, 'Effects of Reiki on Pain, Anxiety, and Blood Pressure in Patients Undergoing Knee Replacement: A Pilot Study', *Holistic Nursing Practice*, 31(2) 2017, 80–89, https://pubmed.ncbi.nlm.nih.gov/28181973/
[36] Goldsby TL, Goldsby ME, McWalters M & Mills PJ, 'Effects of Singing Bowl Sound Meditation on Mood, Tension, and Well-being: An Observational Study', *Journal of Evidence-Based Complementary & Alternative Medicine* 22(3) (2017), 401-406. https://www.ncbi.nlm.nih.gov/pmc/articles/PMC5871151/